Rún buíochais / Thanks

Thanks to Ealaín na Gaeltachta for their continual support of my creative endeavours and for giving me a bursary in 2015 to work on a number of books including this one. Buíochas ó chroí

Thanks to Paddy Bushe and Frank Sewell for their long engagement with my work and for their inspired translations.

Thanks to Mathw Staunton at The Onslaught Press for his dedication, his encouragement and his friendship. I'm delighted to be published by this enterprising press.

Thanks to my lovely godson, Sabal Sapkota, a two year old bundle of joy and wisdom.

Cathal Ó Searcaigh, June 2018

The View from the Glen

Selected Prose by Cathal Ó Searcaigh

with drawings by Ian Joyce

The Onslaught Press

Published by The Onslaught Press
on Midsummer's Day 2018

ISBN: **978-1-912111-54-1**

The texts and titles are set in **Le Monde Livre** by Jean Francois
Porchez with cited poetry in Stanley Morison's **Times**
Printed & bound by Lightning Source

for my godson
Sabal Sapkota

A ray of sunshine
peeped out from the darkness

Homeground

Poetry Matters

Upbringing

1. Homeground

◯

The Language Issue

In the past it was customary for Irish-language writers to be grumpy. They felt marginalized, left out of things. Some disorder or other in the make-up of their metabolism, perhaps, or some collapse in the set-up of their imagination made them become losers. The health food of recognition, when occasionally it came their way, only made them unhealthier. Everything around them seemed to droop and decay. If they had an artificial flower it would surely lose its lustre and die. Roger McGough in a succinct little poem titled 'Missed' seems to allude to them in all their groggy hopelessness: *"Out of work/ divorced/ usually pissed/ they aimed low in life/ and missed."* I'm glad to be of a much more upbeat, optimistic generation of Irish-language writers. As a result of our extravagant positiveness we have moved from the margins to the centre page of popularity. We are no longer the footnotes. We have become the centrefold of notoriety.

We are gods in exile. We have, I believe, the potential to empower ourselves, to be creators of our own cosmos. In the early nineties, I had a rare experience of that kind of heart-swelling ebullience at an Altan concert in Milwaukee. It was an open-air extravaganza with many great groups performing, but Altan with their predominantly Irish-language repertoire stole the show. Introducing their songs and their tunes in Irish they showed an unflinching belief that the Irish language was dashingly cool and daringly hip. As I cast an eye around that vast assortment of people, I could see Shamrock-clad grandmothers from Boston stomping to the thrill and throb of a *strathspey* and ageing Finn McCool hipsters from San Francisco, but with very little hair to hold the proverbial Scott McKenzie flower, all lilting that funky highway reel 'The Glen Road to Carrick'. I got talking to a red-headed black man from the Mississippi Delta who had a passion for "*old motha Ireland and Shane-nose singin', man*". Under the pull and power of Altan that huge crowd became one and I could hear a reeling chorus of heartbeats proclaiming joyously that they were Irish to the innermost boglands of their soul.

That swinging two-hour Gaeltacht created by Altan that night on the shores of Lake Michigan was, for me, a positive experience. It reinforced my belief that Irish, despite talk of its terminal decline, its low-status, marginalized existence, was still a language of awesome power. Hadn't Altan proved by their supercharged performance that they were sustained and nourished by its strength and vigour; that for them it was not an inert endowment from the past but a real source of vitality in the here and now of the present. After the concert was finished, I overheard someone use the term "ethno-futurism" to describe Altan's unabashed belief in their native tongue and their unflinching confidence in its musical culture. "Ethno-futurism" is, I suppose, about taking a spirited stance on one's own ethnic heritage; ensuring that a language and a way of life are given the chance to continue.

Over the past three decades, this corner of Irish-speaking Donegal, where I live, has produced an astounding wealth of musical virtuosity; artists who are affirmative about their native language. Many have become stars in the international music firmament. They blaze as brightly in California as they do in Cois Cladaigh or Caiseal na gCorr. Clannad, Altan, Enya are cherished in Detroit and Dubai as much as they are in Dore. Wherever in the world I find myself, I hear the otherworldly Irish music of these artists being played in public and private places. Whether it's in a ritzy restaurant on Siam Square in Bangkok, or in a goatherd's hut in a remote Himalayan Valley, that music knows no bounds, no borders, no barricades. Like light, it's boundless in its capacity to cross over, to connect.

As a child growing up in the Gort a' Choirce area of North West Donegal in the fifties and sixties, the Irish language was the local community lingo but even then it was in crisis. I remember as a monolingual child of five being brought to the fair day in Falcarragh by my grandfather. Falcarragh, the commercial centre of the parish, is situated about six miles from my ancestral hill-farm in Mín 'a Leá. We went there by bus. What a wondrous journey it was. My grandfather doting on me; the two of us chatting away in Irish. Strolling around in the bazaared dazzle of those fair-day streets I was baffled by my grandfather's speech. He spoke hesitantly and with great difficulty, I thought, in a strange cumbersome language. When I asked him what it was he squatted down beside me, took my small hands in his big knobbly hands, and spoke softly to me in Irish:

"Here we will have to speak English because they will think we're from the bogs."

"But aren't we from the bogs, granda," I piped up with childish innocence."

"You will have to learn English, a chroí, so that the bog can be sifted out of you."

I began to learn that day that with the colonic

irrigation of English we could cleanse ourselves of the build-up of Irish in our gut. I also began to think that all Irish speakers were another branch of the Flintstones; a rather silly stone-age family; a goofy page right out of history. Mín 'a Leá where I lived, meaning 'the plain of flat stones', was, it seemed to me then, the most backward part of Bedrock. I certainly didn't want to be yabba-dabba-doohing in Irish. I didn't want to have any part in the future of our barmy Irish past.

I was getting the message clear and sharp that Irish was a spent force; a backward, anti-modern, parochial language, belonging to another time, another place; and to encourage in any way a widespread use of it would be a stupid isolationist act that would limit our possibilities, narrow our horizons. In the middle of the nineteenth century Daniel O'Connell, the Liberator, stated with enthusiastic assurance, "*Although the Irish language is connected with many recollections that twine around the hearts of Irishmen, yet the superior utility of the English tongue as a medium of all modern communication is so great that I can witness without a sigh the gradual disuse of the Irish.*" Likewise the cynical post-colonial élite continued to discredit the language. For them it was an object of ridicule, the oafish tongue of the bogs. As a young boy I was picking up on all of this and getting the impression that my native language was inferior. I was conditioned to despise my language. It was the tongue of the dispossessed, the language of backwardness.

The Revivalists, many of them redneck fanatics, really added to my belief that the language was crass and dull. These smug, self-appointed defenders of language put a lot of people off Irish. The intimidating presence of these purists—linguistic McCarthyites who inspected your grammar, your syntax, your *blas*—made learners, especially, very self-conscious about speaking the language. Even I who was a native speaker, suffered from an acute tension in my tenses and, sometimes, a severe diarrhoea in my declensions, when these puritanical grammarians were present. When they scrutinised my vowel movements I become sexually awkward with my genitive case.

In my early teens I had a change of heart about the Irish language. The Muse of Poetry beckoned and led me back to Irish. She convinced me that I could be a tuned-in, cosmopolitan and still have strong roots in my *dúchas*. She opened an Irish doorway for me onto the world; a liberating doorway to life.

This change of heart happened in London. I became acutely aware of the word 'home' while I was cruising around Piccadilly Circus, in the mid-seventies: "*a hustle here, a hustle there, hey babe, take a walk on the wild side*." In the amped-up lingo of Lou Reed I was a thrill-seeking teenager, doing my best to be self-indulgently hip. But I was just a foppishly dressed yob from the backcountry.

I felt uneasy being funky and as a result I began to look into that terrible dark pool of the self; the *Duibheagán*, as I call it in Irish. At times like that, you realise you're an abyss, a pitch-black pit. There's only a deep darkness. You get dizzy looking down into the gulf, the chasm of yourself. You realise there's a deadening, deafening silence; that there are no answers. A poem became for me an act of defiance thrown in the face of that silence. I wrote in English, poems of adolescent angst, mostly. A poetry of pimples. I wrote bad poems because I didn't have the humility to read really great ones. Until one evening in the autumn of 1975 a man who worked in the store-room of Oxford University Press walked into the pub where I worked and handed me a copy of Derek Mahon's latest collection, *The Snow Party*. That book had a profound effect on me, especially the first poem, called 'Afterlives'. Derek Mahon, a Belfastman, had gone to London at the beginning of the Northern Troubles and I think he felt it on his conscience that he hadn't accounted for these terrible times in his poetry. So 'Afterlives' is a home-coming poem, in that Mahon came back to Belfast. The last verse was a real shock of recognition.

> But the hills are still the same
> grey blue above Belfast
> perhaps if I stayed behind
> and lived it bomb by bomb
> I might have grown up at last
> and learnt what is meant by home.

Home! The word just winged its way off the page. I felt the word as an intense desire to be reunited with something from which I felt I was cut off from. The word was a smell from another world, the last domain of my *dúchas*. *Dúchas* is a difficult word to explain in English, but briefly it means a connection, a feeling of attachment to a place, a tongue and a tradition, a belief that one belongs to a sustaining cultural and communal energy; that one has a place and a name. Suddenly I realised that I was in exile in an alien city where I neither had a face, nor a name or a place. To be an exile meant to be on my own. It meant to be without the community's sense of warmth and settledness. I had to return home to reclaim my heritage, my *dúchas*. And for me the *dúchas* is not a flight into the past, rather a rejoining of the past, the present and the future. It is a quest, perhaps for an expanded present which flows backwards and forwards with the one and same movement.

Home! The word was a discovery—but what is discovery, only what we remove the cover from. It has always been there—only hidden. I also realised that Irish was my emotional language, and not English. Intuitively, I knew more about the texture and the tone, the aura of words in Irish. The language inhabited my consciousness, perhaps, in a way that English didn't. From then on, I would write poetry in Irish. "She" would connect me to the vital creative energies of my *dúchas*. She would bring me back home.

The language linked me to a wellspring of tribal memories; an archive of ancestral experiences; a library of folk wisdom that was distinctly Irish. I felt that I belonged to something peculiarly enriching; something with its own irreplaceable value system. I was able to assert myself and withstand being absorbed and assimilated into whatever standard was being foisted on me from abroad. Oscar Wilde stated somewhere that "*most people are other people. Their thoughts are someone else's opinions, their lives a mimicry, their passions a quotation.*" The Irish language enables me, I believe, to be uniquely myself. The language allows me to have a distinctively native viewpoint, my own radiant window of wonder onto the world.

I started learning English at the primary school. It was liberating becoming aware of two languages, two different ciphers to denote the same thing. How could *cnoc* be *hill*? I favoured *cnoc* because it sounded more rounded to me. It seemed to fit those bulbously plump swells that surrounded me. *Hill* seemed to me then to be slender, too blunt. It sounded more like an upthrust, a stone pillar. On the other hand I learned that *fridge* was called *cuisneoir* in Irish. We didn't have a fridge at home but I knew what it was from a shop in Gort a' Choirce. It was where they kept ice cream. *Fridge* was an ice-cold box that shut tight with a rubbery, sludgy, snap. *Cuisneoir* I'd never heard as a spoken word, a living word in the month of any local.

When I asked somebody about it they said "*ó sin Gaeilge mhaide na leabhar*". It was a school word and, because of my distaste for school, a dead word. Now I am very fond of *cuisneoir*. It's an apt evocation of the fridge in Gaeilge. It comes from the word *cuisne*, meaning frosty or cold-haze. It's the kind of linguistic adaptability I admire. Using a root word in Irish and extending and enlarging its meanings, its *brí*. *Brí* in Irish signifies *meaning* but also means *strength* and *vigour*. In short, having two languages enabled me to see the world through two different lenses. I came later to realise that each lens was tilted differently. It became apparent that Irish allowed me to see the world in emotional close-up while English provided, for me, a conceptual wide-shot of the world.

Donegal, where I live, is geographically in the North but politically in the South. Personally I like its sort of indeterminate, borderland position. These sorts of places tend to be enigmatic and ambiguous; places where different ideas, different identities, different histories, meet and challenge each other. These places are frontiers. From here we can develop new approaches, explore unknown territories of the imagination. Donegal artists like Brian Friel, Frank McGuinness, Altan and Clannad have all drawn inspiration from the country's frontier-like location. It has conditioned how they have reshaped and renewed the tradition.

I myself live in an area where the interaction between Irish and English is most challenging. It's a linguistic borderland. As Irish-speakers we are adapting and absorbing, aligning our language to the needs and nuances of our time. We listen to *sean-nós* singing on ghetto-blasters made in Japan. We tell stories around our German radiators. You may be a highly esteemed traditional singer totally tapped into the *dúchas* and yet live in a mock-Tudor-thatched-cottage-hacienda. A friend of mine has a libidinous tomcat called Pangur Bán, shaggy from too many prowling erection-packed nights. Another friend had a little soulful-looking mini car called An Bonnán Buí. In my oriental draped kitchen I sometimes sing 'Caoineadh na dTrí Muire' to the air of 'Lady Madonna'. Lovely outrageous ways of repossessing the tradition and breathing new life into it. Traditionalists, who are cocooned in the past, are always fearful of the bold, risk-taking adventure of the present. As Irish-speakers we have to adopt new strategies for the survival of our language in a changing society—adapt ourselves to the multiple cultural realities around us. All the recent statistical studies show that the Gaeltacht, the historical heartland of Irish, is in a state of decline. Personally, I'm inclined nowadays to see the Gaeltacht as a fragmented entity; geographically dispersed across the globe. It is wherever people come together to speak Irish: a gay bar in the Greenwich Village of Gaoth Dobhair; a shopping mall in the Bay Area of San Falcarragh; a sean-nós singing class in the

Muicíneach-Idir-Dhá-Sháile of Monte Carlo; a St. John's *tine chnámh* in the Ceathrú Thadhg of Chicago.

Change is of course a crucial aspect of "life". We live in a flux and ferment where being is eternally in a state of becoming. Consequently, culture is never a fixed, immutable entity—something finished once and for all—that we inherit and preserve. The notion that Irish culture stands motionless in time, perfectly transfixed in the past, is a common belief in our country. I am not at all interested in this myopic view of culture. I'm interested in the creative and transformative possibilities of culture; its abilities to renew itself, to develop and evolve. To be fluid and dynamic, futuristic and forward-looking. Too often we become mesmerised by the past instead of paying attention to the present. It's like driving a car and looking out the rear view mirror instead of the windshield. A deadly practice.

At present, we are expecting convulsions of change in our society; a shifting of boundaries and a reshaping of identities. With increased migration to our shores, we are living in a state of cultural multiplicity, of linguistic diversity; of inevitable hybridity. A time of wandering borders and an overlapping of cultures where it's no longer credible to believe in a single unified identify. Making claims for a pure identity can, as we know too well, create an aggressive polarity between people and lead to a vicious politics of intolerance.

Until recently the feet of many Chinese girls were bound up horrendously to hinder their natural growth. A deeply ingrained cultural perception led to the belief that deformed feet were objects of exquisite beauty. Likewise, living exclusively within a particular ethnic identity can lead to a distorted condition of the mind that skews the vision and warps the outlook. It is necessary to break out of these imposed constructs and establish more relaxed parameters for ourselves.

It is healthy to open up to the uniqueness and the strangeness of other cultures, other ethnic perspectives. We are enriched by their differences, by their diversity.

As Irish-speakers we have to channel the potential and harness the energies of the great rainbow river of culture that is sweeping through our lives. Our great challenge is how to avail of the power of the mainstream, in order to maintain our own small stream.

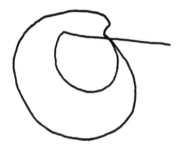

Sense of Place

I

I'm enjoying a quiet, outdoors Sabbath. Alone I make my way through the bog along the sinewy trails of sheep. It's an evening of scudding clouds and murmuring water.

Out here where green life thrives I'm refreshed by birdsong and the scent of honeysuckle. I become attentive to wonders; to the white drift of hawthorn in a hollow, to patchy sunlight on a hill, to the chant of green foliage on Joyce's farm.

I thank an ancient elder tree for its nurturing breath and curtsy in front of a pink rhododendron. I'm grateful to have an intimate place in the midst of this bountiful community of grass, trees and soil.

My senses mingle with their essences. I know that to be is a blessing. In this sacred moment I want all things to be happy. The earth spins, the trees sway in the wind, the light glides along a hilltop, all is alive and all is dance. I pity those who are estranged from the earth. There is nothing more ennobling than to touch and be touched by this beauty.

Bound here between the ether and the abyss, on the edge of edgelessness, I give thanks to this earthly fate for giving me the gift to wonder, to be surprised, to tremble. My salvation is here and not in any other world.

Today my religion is a creed of amplitude; an open heart that asks the branching tree and the tunnelling earthworm for the truth. This clear mountain stream —steadfast, giving, spirited—tells me all I need to know about the Dharma. A moss-covered stone is as edifying as any sacred scripture. In the presence of still lake-water at Loch an Ghainimh I know the revelatory power of silence.

I feel a vibrancy in every atom of my being that brings me into alignment with blazing galaxies and with blades of grass. After all, every particle of my body comes from that primordial orgasm of matter that begot the universe. I'm an exudation of that primal energy. Today it flows through me with an aching love to coalesce, to be whole again. Every part of me and every part of you, every grain of sand and every blade of grass, contains a configuration of the whole. All living matter, be it minute protozoa or a supernova, is intertwined in the bounteous weave of creation. Seán Ó Riordáin, the Irish-language poet, recognized this cosmic dynamic in a poem called 'Ní Ceadmhach Neamhshuim'. *"Nil aon áit ar fud na cruinne nach ann a saolaíodh sinne"* (there's nowhere in the universe where we have not been born), is, I think, one of his most visionary insights.

We live in grim times. The intricate balance in nature, that interweave of parts, is coming undone. In the name of development, economic growth and progress, we are all complicit in the ecological holocaust that is laying waste to our world. Countless species are being wiped out, radioactive waste and toxic exhausts foul our waters and spoil our air. The detritus of prosperity, the effluent of greed, is killing the earth. Only when we become one ecological congregation, a wholehearted fellowship of love, swearing allegiance to the branching tree and the tunnelling earthworm, will we bring the earth and ourselves back into a natural alignment of needs.

Lucky for me I can enjoy a quiet, outdoors Sabbath in a place where the ecosystem is still diverse and thriving. For that I am grateful. As morning dawns and as evening darkens, I give praise for the bright spill of light that allows me to see the unfolding universe of wonder that is Mín 'a Leá, Mín na Craoibhe and Caiseal na gCorr.

II

I'm writing this on a Sunday evening as a soft velvety dusk hugs the hills. The glen is awash in a glow of purple. I'm more in tune with this lovely twilight of blackbird, lark and cuckoo than I am with the cacophony of a city and its stammering orchestra of bass-tuba traffic. In this open space I have a Freedom to look, listen and dream. In this rural amplitude I give my soul to my senses.

Drawing water from the well a wee while ago I watched the sun creep across the hills. Like returning cows I heard the brown bogs low contentedly in the declining light. Being of these hills I want nothing more than to hold this landscape in my arms, stroke its ruddy cheeks of heather, smell the gorse in its hair, kiss its evening eyes.

I like to think of myself as a citizen of the green constituency of the wild.

Whatever about this ruling government in Dublin I have my very own thrilling assembly in the garden, my Dáil of Warblers, my Senate of grasshoppers whose governance is clear and lucid; a green supremacy of song. Marcus Thrush Aurelius, my emperor of dawn and dusk, holds sway on the hedgerow, delighting me with his well-tuned truths. Here everything is ratified by song.

Now, earth and sky merge and blend. Soon, I will hear the stars chirping like crickets in the lea-fields of the sky.

A millennium ago a Chinese poet remarked, "*a thousand years may be beyond me but I can turn this moment into an eternity*".

Poised above an Eachla Mhór the quarter moon is a beautiful ear. I let whoops of delight.

*****

I am a devotee of Li Po and Tu Fu, two seers of the T'ang dynasty. I love the clear-sighted clarity of their poems. They remind me of light through doors, the light thrown out of houses on winter evenings at dusk when the doors are still slightly ajar. The wealth of that light, especially in the hilly townlands where I live, where the houses are few and far between, has always been inviting. The spill of light from these poems is what draws me in.

I am also reading Mary Oliver, a poet who looks at things with the same clear-sighted Chinese attentiveness as the T'ang poets. Silence is brought acutely to speech in her poems, sparingly and patiently. She has the knack to flip the common phrase and make it spin with a brand-new, guinea-bright shininess, giving it a lovely currency of clarity. She is an activator of the common phrase, finding in it a source of mystery and a subtlety of melody that delights me to the full, throbbing end of my coccyx. Like Mary Oliver, I'm a born-again pastoralist and proud of it.

These mornings, I'm wakened early by the scent of flowering shrubs. I'm keen to live in the present. Too many people live life as if it were a rehearsal, a try-out, a dry run for the real thing, the authentic life to come further down the road. The urgency of the moment, the shock of the now is more potent to me than the promise of the future. "*Jump into experience while you are alive*", Kabir, the Indian mystic poet, urged his followers. I believe in beginning my journey anew each day.

I have lucid moments in my garden, luminous ones, even.

> FUSCHIA
> You're the talk of the garden,
> you with your purple knickers
> in full view of the fern —
> that rigid bishop
> with his crozier.
>
> ROSES
> Country girls from the 1940s
> you stand at my gable

flounced up and in bows
and give me the eye
soft as a cow.

HYDRANGEA
Midday, such stifling heat,
the hydrangea by the wayside
flops down and drowses—
an old lady laden
with blue shopping bags

Some people are so hardened, so tough-skinned, so rhinocerized, that, as Eugene Ionesco said, a single flower wouldn't grow on them. I favour poets who flower in and out of season.

I would also concur with Joe Gould, the legendary down-and-out Greenwich Village sage, who said that the best path to enlightenment was to be a Buddhist in winter and a nudist in summer. That means to be truly alive to the beat and thump, the flow and tempo of your own being.

In the light of what I have been saying these are my guidelines to open up, to become a willing participant in the joyful mysteries of the here and now.

—*Be a seer. Take notice of ripples of light and the drift of smoke.*
—*Don't give anyone the cold shoulder. Befriend bugs.*
—*Open out. Have a bawdy chat with a wild flower. Flirt with a pansy.*

—*Religious texts are surrealist manifestos. Smile in church.*
—*An old garden in the moonlight. That's your doorway to the marvellous.*
—*Once a week be a bed of rumpled pleasures.*
—*Listen to megalithic rumbles from your past. The Stone Age is still in your genes. Let the spirit of things reveal themselves to you. Listen to the song of stones.*
—*Improvise. Be a slinky jazz-tune, avoid jaded kisses and shrivelled smiles. Joy is portable. Carry it always.*

—*Allow birdsong into your talk. Your words will become more tender.*
—*Plant an apple tree even if it's the end of the world.*
—*Listen to your heart as if it were a diva in your private opera.*
—*Be a brent goose. Migrate.*
—*Keep loose. Don't let institutions wall you in.*
—*Acquaint yourself with Death. Study gravestones.*
—*Throw away the road-maps. Follow your ley-lines.*

III

We overlook the wonders that surround us, the neighbouring worlds of nature.

Birds, beasts, plant life, the mineral domain, they are also our close kin who share the same earth with us. We are as much animal, vegetable, mineral as we are human. We are all carbon kindred, an intermingling family of the same stock element. It's a lineage that binds all living matter inasmuch as blood binds kith and kin.

We are in our element, so to say, when we align ourselves to their familiar presences, to their energies. You are never alone when you acknowledge and appreciate the presence of these intimates. I know that for some the angst of being alone and apart is indeed very real—a deep-seated lonesomeness, arising from a firm belief that we are all separate entities. I lean towards the idea of shared origins, a familiar carbon ethnicity that binds us and yet lets us be boundless.

On my daily walks around the glen I open up and enjoy the spirited communion of being a participant in this vibrant world. I'm ceaselessly surprised by the wild diversity flourishing around me. And I'm constantly being lifted, emotionally and imaginatively, beyond my own enclosed life into the life of all, into immense existence.

What sights and what sounds? I will see a higgledy parade of thistles by the wayside or, maybe, a nervy rabbit crouching in the rushes. A far-off farm lit up in a splash of light—or a red dangle of fuchsia—will brighten my way.

I'll tingle with joy at a white glissade of swans on Loch an Ghainimh. I will breathe in the honey-suckle's sweet exhalation in Caiseal na gCorr. I'll marvel at the collusions of sunset colours above Carn Traona, a grand wreckage of amber and violet, ivory and gold, ochre and oyster, blazing across the sky.

I will be close to the click and tap of a wren in a dry-stone wall and to a robin with its little song aquiver in the winter twigs. I will be alert to buds greening on a spring branch, and to a quartz rock resplendent on a sunny hillside.

I will greet the leafy tongue of grasses; respond to the grope of roots, to the sharp bristle of a briar, to the abrupt stir of a moorhen, to a mousy bat foraging in the dark.

I will find peace at the Dúloch, watching a Milky Way of water-lilies stretching across the stellar silence of its waters. And I will attend to my own salvation, not by submitting to the words or beliefs of others but by attuning myself to the deep humming of bees in the flowering heather of Mín 'a Leá; to the fraternity of mosses at Páirc Mheabha; to the hawthorn on Andy's Farm, a profligate of joy, bridal-white in summer, berry-red in winter; to the chant of wind across the acres of wild bog in Altan; to rainlight, to cloudswirls, to sunspots.

Seeing the forthright authority of a lone ash-tree, the spontaneity of daisies and the patience and resolve of a bog asphodel, I will feel blessed to be a part of this planetary community, this largeness of life.

I know that if I act in consonance with it I will always have this bountiful experience. And I will live generously.

IV

Creativity, for me, arises to a large extent out of my deep attachment to my home place and out of a reverential affection for my people. My poems are devotional in the sense that they are prayerful celebrations of place, tongue and tradition.

My work has become known, I believe, because of its connectedness with a particular place; a beautiful mountain valley at the foot of Mount Errigal in northwest Donegal, Ireland. I have become the collector of its oral traditions, the archivist of its memories and myths, the narrator of its story maps. In this role, I am like the Gaelic, bardic poets of the past, recording and registering what is past or passing.

I use place names a lot in my poems. The sense of place, the sacredness of place, is a common motif in Irish poetry. For me, there's an urgency to name things. This comes from a sense of crisis. The place names are being forgotten. This happens more in my area as the Irish language shrinks and the English language spreads. It's so sad, this communal amnesia. This detailed naming of the land that my people did was their way of transforming the wilderness into a place where they could feel at home. In this manner, they domesticated the raw landscape and imposed meaning upon the wildness.

I love these names because of the linguistic heritage and the cultural experience encapsulated in them. For me, these names are sources of historical memories, vital transmitters of the tales and traditions of my people's past. For a lot of people, nowadays, the landscape is silent. They no longer have the name to invoke the spirit of a place. You can't converse properly with a hill, a field, a hollow or a rock without addressing it by its name. Poetry for me is a means of making memorable what is being forgotten. The continual enumeration of place names in my poetry is a way of gathering the past into the present, hoping that there will be a future for that past. 'Caiseal na gCorr Station', for example, is a poem dealing with these preoccupations.

AT CAISEAL NA gCORR STATION

Here at Caiseal na gCorr Station
I tracked my own secluded place,
my sanctuary, and my escape.
Here I am on the one note
with what's in me, what's around me.
Here I can feel my roots
as I survey the territory of my people

around the foot of Errigal
where they are three centuries settled
on the grassy hill-pastures
from Mín 'a Leá to Mín na Craoibhe.
Here, spread out before me
just like an open book, is the whole wide range
from Doire Chonaire to Prochlais.
Above me and below, I see the holdings
that were wrested from the jaws of wilderness.
This is the anthology of my people,
the manuscript they laboured over
with their sweat for ink.
Here every field is a stanza
in the great poem of cultivation.
Now I read this epic of determination
in the green vernacular of the holdings
and it is no more or no less than *pietas*
when I throw down my challenge to nothingness
as my people wrestled with their wilderness
until their grit and doggedness
earned them their due.
Here I feel poetry *can* make something happen.
I feel the stir of meaning, of my own meaning
pulsing to the heartbeat of my people.
And all of this overcomes desire, gentles thought,
dissolves the irreconcilable in the here and now.

—*translated by Paddy Bushe*

At Caiseal na gCorr Station I'm reminded of my
dúchas. Some words defy translation and *dúchas* is
one of them. It's a labyrinth of lexical ramifications.
For Irish language speakers, it means the cultural
endowment that we receive from our people's past.
At Caiseal na gCorr, I sense that the *dúchas* is not an

inert endowment but a living source of vitality. It's my task as a poet to channel it into a new permanence.

At Caiseal na gCorr, I become mediumistic to a certain extent in that I let the old generation speak through me. Perhaps it's easier to do this in Ireland than elsewhere. The ever-present presence of the past is always with us in Ireland. The past is not disposed of, as we might expect. It is in a very special way still here and still alive. Somehow, it has entered the here and now so that it never dies; however thickly the grass grows over it. At Caiseal na gCorr, I have become aware that my community extends not only in place but also in time; that all those who died in these hill-farming townlands are not remote figures in the dead past but a part of my own flesh and blood. This is what Seamus Heaney called "*a genealogical imagination*". Like Seamus, I, too, come from a race of storytellers, sages who handed down an incomparable oral tradition of song and story, of tribal memories.

Maybe that's why I am drawn so much back into my racial past. We all, I believe, have a nostalgia for origins. Anyway, life, as Nietzsche so aptly observed, is lived forwards but understood backwards.

V

For a lot of us the only way to read the literature of other cultures is through the medium of translation. It would be a terrible loss if we couldn't get some sense of the great writers in languages different from our own. This makes the task of translation a crucial cultural undertaking. Some people, especially in Irish, are very worried about fidelity in translation, about straying from the original. The literal version to them is sacred. But as Stanley Kunitz so rightly pointed out, *"even a literal version is already a radical reconstitution of the verbal ingredients of a poem into another linguistic system"*. Arthur Waley noted *"There are seldom sentences that have word for word equivalents in another language. It becomes a question of choosing between various approximations."*

In order to be a good translator one must understand that each language has its own unique register, its own peculiar world-view. Certain cultures, I believe, speak less than others. They are semantically sullen, you could say. Others delight in linguistic ornamentation. They exult in exaggeration. They take great pleasure in large gestures of language, excessive movement of words. Rhetorical utterance, for instance, is absolutely convincing in Irish-language poetry. But we respond to modem poetry in English differently. The kind of exuberance we find in Irish is awkward to the current register of English. It's harsh on the ear in English. We have to modify the amplification level. That's why it's important for the translator to be attuned to the register of both the original and the target language.

This has been brought home to me on numerous occasions when confronted with translations of my own poems into English. I have a poem that l wrote for my father. In the poem—an early one of mine—I walk the streets of London thinking about him. I envy how content he is within the narrow limits of his poor hill-farm. The poem ends with these lines:

> Ach tá mé gan an dúthracht chiúin
> a chloígh do scealp is seascann dúr
> is tá mé mar chách ag séanadh gnáis
> faoi bhuarach báis na sráide.

'*Buarach*' means *spancel* or *chain*. According to Dinneen '*buarach báis*' means "*an unbroken hoop of skin cut with incantation from a corpse, across the entire body from shoulder to footsole and wrapped in silk of the colours of the rainbow and used as a spancel to tie the legs of a person to produce certain effects by witchcraft*".

All of that sub-textual lore is contained in the Irish word, but how does a translator manage to evoke even a hint of it. Frank Sewell, an insightful translator of my poems, accomplished this task wondrously:

> But I lack the quiet devotion
> to take on rock and bog
> Like everyone else l swap customs
> for street cred and newer gods.

This is not a reproduction of the poem in English. It's a reconstitution of it. Its aim is to show something of what the original poem had—how it breathed, its cadences, the stress and pitch of it.

I'm eager to know who's writing in Ghana, what poets are coming to the fore in Papua New Guinea, who's voicing dissent in Tehran, what Rimbaud is blazing a trail in Urdu. Only for translation I wouldn't have a finger on the pulse of world poetry.

FOR MY FATHER

I thought of him last night
in the rat-race of the street.
How he never took to the city's
short shrift and cool conceit.

I was struck by his conversation,
a chip off the ancient block,
and when I made with it this prayer,
a blind alley turned its back.

He smiled under the strain
of his usual up-hill graft;
and I envied the strange dignity
of his stern, unworldly craft.

But I lack the quiet devotion
to take on rock and bog.
Like everyone else, I swap customs
for street cred and newer gods.

—*translated by Frank Sewell*

VI

Ian Joyce is my neighbour in Mín 'a Leá and an artist of international standing.

He is someone who sees the abyss at his feet and yet manages to continue.

His landscapes take exciting risks, a silent daring to summon up and reveal the mystic reality of the familiar. This is not a banal venture into Blakean transcendentalism. In his landscapes Ian Joyce commutes with the common place in a way that is neither trite nor predictable. He is a visionary of the real, a see-r who liaises with what is marvellous in the ordinary.

Whether it is a picture of an angel marooned on a wild twilit moor, a bog ablaze with Autumn or a moon delicate as a seedling in an April sky, the ethereal is always conveyed with a close, earthy actuality.

A recent painting of Ian's hangs in my house. The luxuriant yellow of a sunny evening in Fána Bhuí fills my room with an other-worldly brilliance. It shines with light, the kind of lustre that surrounds old saints and mystics, the glow of icons.

Like Wendell Berry, a sublime poet of the great American outdoors who buries his cast-aside winter writings in the earth come Springtime so that the old commingles with the new and the past submits to the future, Ian Joyce uses his rejected jottings and his abandoned diaries as calligraphic components in his art, thus fusing the past with the future.

Using a light solvent and brushing it across page after page of the written minutiae of his life, his personal archive is washed out and defaced. However it is a transformative act where the text is given an afterlife; a slow release of something other than its original intention. A veiled life of rare visual patterns is elicited from the ruins and residues of the faded pages, graphic fragments that transmit past truths, perhaps, or future presentiments.

It is also, I think, an attempt to free language from its weighty load of linguistic sense and give it a new visual coherence. This approach gives his art the appearance of archaic tablets, ancient fragments of a language aglow with the lore of fresh beginnings.

Whatever linguistic traces remain are transmuted into graphic runes. A *rúnscríbhinn* beautiful as the hieroglyphics of winter ice on bog holes. It is the inscrutable speech of things; the hoarse cry of the wind across March hills; the moist, salty tongue of dripping rain; the cosmic pulse of stones.

It is also a speechlessness in the face of suffering. In a number of his large-scale installations Ian Joyce identifies with those who suffer under oppressive regimes. His homage to Jan Palach, a young Czech student who set himself alight in public as a protest against the Soviet occupation of his country in 1968; an act of self-immolation that stunned the world, shows exactly where the artist's sympathies lie. This major installation is a suspended sculptural print that uses written material from Ian's own personal history but he violates the text as an act of self-effacement. Although an anonymity is given to the text this only amplifies its truth. Encrypted within these defaced pages is the artist's outrage against any authoritarianism. It is a work of bearing witness. By mourning Jan Palach he is also lamenting the voice-less dead of all despotic regimes. This is not an indulgent art that is created for a purely aesthetic end and Ian Joyce is not a self-righteous spokesperson for suffering humanity. He knows full well that either a lofty aesthetic or a moralizing simplicity can give offence to suffering. He also knows that art should not be used to lull us into a state of self-contented pity. Although art cannot alleviate suffering it can draw attention to it, create a compassionate awareness around it and thereby become a vehicle of socio-political change.

In his 'Archive for Jan Palach' and more recently in his 'Shroud for Mohamed Bouazizi', the young Tunisian who set the Arab world ablaze after making an inferno of himself, Ian Joyce reaches out imaginatively to those afflicted by tyranny and heavy-handed ideologies. In his art he is firmly on the side of singularity, separateness and free-thinking individualism, values that are anathema to repressive regimes.

VII

I always loved the lure and the lore of the open road; taking to the highways and the byways, the tracks, the paths and the trails without a mapped-out strategy, just a giddy itinerary of aimlessness.

Of course I've been privileged to have a certain amount of leisured freedom to indulge in this delightful vagabondage.

The allure of the unknown has a pulling power that draws me to old lanes and tracts and pathways.

I'm very conscious of the fact that each path has a story to tell.

Every path is a passage between people and place, a communal storyline that connects the past with the present.

A path is the imprint of human history on the landscape, be it a famine road, a pilgrim trail, a turf track, a family lane, a right of way, a nature walk.

I'm always curious about their origins. I like to be in step with those waymakers of the past.

Their footprints are the footnotes of a bygone time; as strange and as intriguing to me as an Ogham inscription.

I become absorbed in their topographies, their ups and downs, their restless meanderings, their stubbornness, their forwardness, their links, their turn offs.

I want to know about their flora and fauna, their geological heritage, their human lineage.

I like to think of these old paths as being patrician, the aged lineaments of the landscape. I become a carrier of their stories, a pedlar of their lore.

VIII

He was suffering, he said, from the harsh weather of the heart.

A change of climate is what he needs — or better still, a change of heart.

I stroked a stone that was shaggy with lichen. It purred.

Going out to walk is a going in to wonder. A sight-seeing tour of the Self.

Sheltering under a Maytime hawthorn, the silky vellum of its blossoms makes me want to write beautifully.

Just now an arrowhead of wild geese dipped and honked across a wintry sky.

And suddenly I'm lying in bed, listening to these same flapping wings and that eerie, wheeling cry across the nightskies of my childhood.

Yesterday we had the rarefied blue of a holiday brochure sky. Today a damp newspaper of grey mist hangs over everything.

Sheep tracks across a tawny autumn bog. I'll follow them. Each pathway has something unique to teach me if only I'm alert enough to pick it up.

In stormy weather I like to walk on exposed paths. Daunting it may be but it's also invigorating. The slap of rain and the whip of wind is bracing. And it always brightens up, even momentarily and I get a chance to smooch with the Light.

There are no maps, she said, to navigate the *terra incognito* of the mind.

I suggested that she read the work of mystic poets.

They are the true pioneers of inner travel: the Pathfinders of the psyche.

Blisters and bliss!

IN AN ALTAN TWILIGHT
after Jerzy Harasymowicz
for Jimmy Simmons, poet (1933-2001),
who loved to Jazz things up

When the sun set
beyond the hills
you could see
in the half-light
the brown piano cows
grazing
in the bogs
between Prochlais and Altan,

filthy dirty,
messing about in the mud
and the mire
among the frogs.

You'd hear
in the march stillness
the oozy moo
of their concertos
the sludgy tramp
of their marches, the moist keening
of their nocturnes
all udderly
out of tune.

You'd see
their pointed ears
listening enthralled
to the frogs' jazz—
to their rhapsodies
in blue raucousness,
their throaty improvisations

in the sleaze
of an Altan bog hole.

After that bog-drenched
holiday
it was a terrible scandal
when they lay down
cowishly
in a concert hall,
braddy cows
at the musical milking

and looked indifferently
at the bog cotton faces
of the gasping audience,
at the fumbling pianists
trying to pull
at the keyboard of their udders,

at the hoo-ha
of the attendants
trying to get them
upright on their feet,
trying to get them
to be grand again.

—translated by the author

IX

From the top of the Trosc as the mist lifts, a veined
landscape comes to light, delicate as the underside
of a sycamore leaf; a gleaming wetness of ruts and
cuts furrowing the terrain between townlands.

A green domesticated glen flanked by tawny autumn bogs runs to the sea.

This is my ancestral home, the hillfarmed holdings of my people.

Here I have a face, a name and a place. I belong to a sustaining communal and cultural energy.We all have a longing to belong, a need for meaning, a yearning for love and as we age a wish for mental calmness. Being part of this close-knit community gives me that affecting sense of well-being; a glad-dening relationship with myself and a warming one with others.

This morning from the heights of An Trosc I think about those delicate channels of communion, physical, emotional, psychic that criss cross this human landscape, connecting people and place in a subtle web of kinship; an intricate grid of roads and paths and lay lines, social conveyance of ties and bonds and associations.

How like the human body this landscape is in its dynamic, in its complex mesh of energy. Long before William Harvey (1578–1657), an English physician, discovered that blood circulated in the veins (and was not, as they thought at the time, absorbed as food) the ancient East knew that a network of subtle channels allowed pranic energy to flow around the body.

The meridians of Chinese acupuncture, the chakraic centres of Yogic consciousness, and the humourlike conduits of ayurvedic medicine attest to this deep understanding of energy circulation in the body and also a clear realization that imbalances and blockages of this dynamic flow cause ailments of the body and illnesses of the mind.

All these ancient therapeutic systems view the body as a network of energies and the healing of it involves setting free trapped energy and letting that current of vitality restore the person to health. Those ancient holistic approaches makes complete sense to me as curative recourses to a whole range of human illnesses both of the body and the mind. It's energizing the body to cure itself. Likewise the earth is a living organism with its own subtle energy lines which protect, sustain and nourish it.

Older belief systems, especially the Goddess cults, were much more attuned to this living earth than present-day religions and were heedful of its needs. The Judeo-Christian Islamic theologies are all human-centred and devoid of any specific ethics of ecology. In Exodus 34:13 there is the command: "*You shall destroy their images and cut down their groves*"; an authoritative call to do away with the wooded sanctuaries of the Goddess.

The Hindu-Buddhist code of beliefs encourages a more venerable communion with the natural world, an acknowledgement of inter-dependence and a sense of the elemental being sacramental.

Ours is a very destructive mind-set, our voracious appetite for economic growth threatens survival. The ruthless exploitation of the natural world and its resources is leading to global ecocide. Impending doom lurks in the murky shadows of Prosperity.

The greed of the free-market creates the need for a non-stop consumerism. We are locked into that all-consuming system that urges us: "*Buy and be Happy*".

Subliminal advertising prescribes it ceaselessly. It is, of course, a nonsense premise that all this conven- ience merchandise makes you better, more fulfilled and happier.

Your personal growth, your worth, your well-being can not, and should not, be quantified by your buy- ing power. Power, prestige, property in themselves will not make you happy.

Only when your outer self is in tune with your inner being, when your head is in harmony with your heart will you find true contentment. And then you will not need this wasteful flow of goods and gadgets to gratify you. You will be replete in your own Self.

Economic growth is about being productive, lucrative, bankable; it's about a ceaseless output of produce. And the more we produce the more we deplete the resources of the Earth. And we create a contagion of waste.

We have maltreated and maimed Gaia, our mother earth. We have convulsed her pranic life-lines, we have disordered her abilities to cleanse, heal and re-energize herself.

Human nature! We have to take stock of these two worlds, know that they are inter-dependent, realize that neither can thrive without being in harmony with the other. Respect for the human, reverence for the earth, these principles should be enshrined in all State and Church ethics.

We also need our economics to be attuned to ecology. Here, however, time still moves slowly, the enduring values of a seasonal, cyclic calendar gives meaning to life. You get a sense of a community being connected to the natural world, to their traditions and to themselves. It s a continuity that I find heartening.

As I look back at the Trosc, it's sitting in a steady yogic posture in the sun, surveying our comings and goings with inscrutable calmness.

X

I'm reading William Wordsworth (l770–l850). Other than the occasional dip into his work over the years I have not read him closely since schooldays.

After days in the "harsh and grating" roar of Dublin I come back to my own house fatigued and faint. Reading him in the hush of my room and hearing the soft roll and swell of his words replenishes me.

I'm charmed and calmed by the lofty grandeur of 'Tintern Abbey'. I read it out aloud. The sonorous beauty of his blank verse, the expressive mantric power of it! The pastoral setting is, of course, beguiling after the "*din of towns and cities*", but it is the sheer uplifting thrust of the words that makes my spirit soar.

Common words given a fresh charge and lift so that they glow and reach new heights of harmony. So that they say the unsayable.

Wordsworth wrote from a Christian outlook and I think it fair to say that his entire aesthetic is closely aligned to the moral precepts of that belief system. The least successful poems for me are those where I detect the "tut-tut" sermonizing of a clergyman. Preachy admonishments may have been acceptable to readers of poetry in Wordsworth's day but in our age of disbelief such writ and warrant effects only demean the poem.

Aldous Huxley remarked that Wordsworth *"pumped the landscape full of Anglicanism"*. But the fulsome, acclamatory speech of 'Tintern Abbey' goes beyond the restraints of any formal religion. It seems to me to be a pantheistic chant to the primitive, creedless power that permeates the cosmos.

It speaks to us with *"nature's universal tongue"*, to use a John Clare phrase. In sentiment I find it closer in its understanding to the Buddhist idea of an eternal energy that pulses through everything; an interlinking force that connects all destinies in the sentient field of Being.

> A motion and a spirit, that impels
> All thinking things, all objects of all thought,
> And rolls through all things.

"God has no religion," as Gandhi remarked. Writing about experiencing God in the world was never an easy task. In 'Tintern Abbey' Wordsworth shuns any stiff, ethical pronouncements or tough, stubborn moralizing in favour of a rapturous humanism.

In this poem he is a hagiographer of nature, extolling its purifying virtues, its transformative powers. It is a moving, persuasive, inspiring statement and it pulls me in again and again with its hypnotic speech; that assured accumulation of sound that lifts me right out of myself, out beyond "the fretful stir" of my own mind.

In many ways I prefer 'Tintern Abbey' to 'Intimations of Immortality' because in its impulse it is more intuitive than discursive. It undoubtedly has strong Christian presuppositions but somehow the poem transcends creed and achieves an imaginative Truth greater in its certitude and conviction—at least for me—than any doctrinaire beliefs.

It has an expressive charisma that charms me to the heights; a buoyancy of speech, a vigour of thought and a spellbinding drive to the Absolute. What more can a poem achieve?

The Lyrical Ballads of 1798 and its reissue in 1802 with the groundbreaking Preface shifted English poetry away from the restrained Augustinian elegance of Pope to a new confidence in the common phrase; from the heroic couplet with its dry glitter of gaudiness to a heady speech forged in the passions of the heart.

Wordsworth, and his great contemporaries, Byron, Coleridge, Shelley and Keats, ushered in a new and fresh relationship between poetry and speech. They gave common speech a lusty, Shakespearean grandeur. They loosened it from the cerebral and aligned it with the heart. And in my room I luxuriate "*in that mighty world of eye and ear*".

Wordsworth was only twenty-eight years old when he wrote this in 1798.

What an achieved style, and what distilled wisdom,
at such a young age.

I bow
to Thee
bright Spirit

who lifts
me up
who fills me

the length
and breadth
of Being

with bright
shining
Life

To be
is a gift
of Light.

I live in the townland of Mín 'a Leá

I live in the townland of Mín 'a Leá. Errigal looms in the background, an upthrust of glinting grey. I suppose you could call it a shape-shifter. Sometimes it's elegant in a cashmere of cloud, other times it's dazzling in a negligee of snow. Sometimes it can be imperially male in a grey gabardine of rain. At other times it can be endearingly homely in a russet brown homespun of heather. It's a witnessing presence to our fleeting lives. My people have survived here for many generations, small hill farmers, struggling but singing. "*Tig críoch ar an tsaol,*" they would say, "*ach mairfidh ceol agus gaol.*" The world may end, but love and music will endure.

Mín 'a Leá is situated at the top of Gleann an Átha, a gently sloping river valley that dips downwards to the sea at Gort a' Choirce.

In my childhood this glen was tilled and cultivated. As a child I loved its picture-postcard prettiness, its cultivated settledness. Nowadays people are no longer working the land here. That era of tillage is now long gone.

The European Economic Union agronomics and its severe ruling has dictated the demise of small crofts. The E.E.U. favours large scale agribusiness, specialized production techniques and a marketplace agronomy. These overbearing agrarian policies finished off subsistence hill-farming here in Gleann an Átha. Faceless bureaucrats in Brussels are inured to the far-reaching effects of their harsh, high-handed policies.

In a poem called 'The Errigal Road', John Montague has these lines:

> All around shards of a lost tradition
> Soon all our shared landscape will be effaced.

These lines are apt and timely to what is happening here in my home place. A lot of the lovely farmlands of my childhood are reverting back to their raw origins, to their primeval bogginess. The wilderness is laying into and clawing back with a vengeance what had been domesticated into neat fields and orderly farms. The starved soil of much of these neglected farmlands has become infected by an epidemic of rushes, thorns and thistles. This is especially true of the *"bailte bánaithe na mbun-chnoc"*, the deserted townlands of the foothills, where this wild contagion of scrub suffocates the frail hillside holdings.

As I get older I find this rural dereliction more and more dispiriting. I mourn it in my poems, the passing away of a particular hill farming culture with its old customs, its distinct language and its compact sense of community. A whole accumulation of wisdom gone to earth!

I have become even more aware of it in the last year since I became the only native dweller left in Mín 'a Leá, the last of the old Gaelic stock left amongst a scattering of mostly English-speaking incomers.

I'm not unaware of the paradox of my situation. I'm someone would broods but doesn't breed.

When I was growing up in Mín 'a Leá in the 1950's and the 1960's everybody was engaged in subsistence farming. It wasn't an easy life, yoked to the soil, trying to make a living on these peaty hill farms. Everybody scrimped and scraped to survive. People were frugal and thrifty. Neighbourliness was an invaluable asset, people helped each other through the bad times. They shared what they had and halved what they didn't have, so to speak. People had their doors open for each other.

It was also a valley of squinting windows. An obsessive inquisitiveness about each other made people peep and snoop. The backbiters had a good sense of rumour. If they thought you were rising above your station, becoming a high-flier, they would soon deflate the balloon of your ego with a sharp pronged put-down.

There was no crime other than minor infringements. Someone would steal a spade or there would be a fistfight over bog rights. Sheep, cows and hens that strayed beyond their bounds were often the culprits in causing rifts between neighbours.

The community was like a spider's web. Everything and everybody in it was intimately interconnected. If you seriously transgressed by pulling a thread here, the jerk of that misdeed, the knock of that offense, would reverberate throughout the entire communal network. Your actions would have repercussions. You would get the cold shoulder from the community. There was nothing more ignominious or more crushing than to lose one's *cliú*, one's social standing among your people. Nobody wanted to be shunned or snubbed, to be an outcast in a tight-knit *pobal* like this. The *pobal* set standards of conduct, models of behavior, certain yardsticks that outlined acceptable actions and attitudes. If you were born and reared here, you understood all of this instinctively. It was in the air, it got transmitted to you by some subtle social osmosis.

There is still a strong sense of community here in Gleann an Átha, a heartening rural camaraderie and co-operation. The only thing threatening it, strange to say, is our own much improved way of life, our steady climb to prosperity. I have always noticed that when people become well off they demand the privileges of privacy. They become withdrawn. They migrate to their own private inner spaces. This can endanger the sort of open, fluid sinuous style of interaction that we have practiced in Gleann an Átha for many a generation. May a door of kindness be always open in our hearts.

I like to walk the russet brown uplands under the benign horse face of an Eachla Mhór. I'm drawn to this remote area, to the deserted townlands of its foothills, to Mín na gCopóg, to Prochlais, to Mín na bPoll.

I'm moved by their green untended pastures fringed by the browns and purples of the bog; their crumbling houses draped in brambles; their small gardens buried in scrub willows; the passage of evening light across their abandoned fields and thistle meadows.

The loneliness and the hopelessness of these wiped-out townlands touch me. What were once busy settlements are now devoid of people. At nightfall where lights once beckoned from hillside houses there is only the gloom of dark.

In the sense that it lacks the living it is a landscape of absence and yet it is not without its presences. A residue of past lives still resides in the rushy fields and the empty houses.

Here, I'm drawn back to roots and sources; to gaping windows and stony hearths; to distant forbears; to ties of kin; to shared experiences. Here, I want to break the ground of forgetfulness, chop up the rooty soil of memory, reclaim bygone lives. Here I am haunted by my people's past, by what is hoarded in the layered earth of their labours.

Sometimes it seems to me that their stories, the spirit of their lives, the lore of what is lost fills the air like a pulse, like a heartbeat.

Suddenly something out of the past stirs, shows signs of life, becomes palpable. It may only be speck-lings of sunshine moving across lost meadows or dappled light along grassy lanes but it's enough to quicken the imagination, to rouse it into utterance.

In that fanciful state I hear snatches of talk at the corner of a field, a man levering stones out of gravelly ground, a child at play, a woman haranguing a dog in the distance. All, it seems, the earth-rooted leavings of past lives.

Subtle, faint, shadowy they arise, the transfigured forbears of these townlands. In Mín na gCopóg, in Prochlais, in Mín na bPoll they still haunt their old familiar holdings. A mere illusion, you say, but I like to believe that a timeless commonwealth of ancestral memories live on and endure, a subtle configuration of consciousness that coexists with us on a parallel plane. And sometimes by pure chance we broach these realms, these domains of future past and like Kavanagh we know that we have walked through fields that were part of no earthly estate.

This hillside neighborhood where I live is full of the carcasses of old abandoned houses left to Time's slow mouldering ruin. Nobody here wants to obliterate a site still occupied by the spirit of the forefathers. These houses may be crumbling ruins but people sense the ancestral presences still hovering around the empty hearths. They firmly believe that it would bring bad luck to knock them down deliberately.

The tribal taboos, particularly in rural Ireland, helped to conserve a considerable amount of our ancient past; raths, fairy rings, megalithic sites, wells. These repositories of prehistory survived because of a sense of ancestral reverence coupled with a fear of the consequences if one violated a venerable site. I accept that attitudes are changing now and people generally are no longer constrained by these notions of ancestral worship. But here where I live the native community still honours these old beliefs.

A ruin that is of great interest to me is the first habitation, supposedly, in Mín 'a Leá. I'm going by hearsay rather than by historical evidence. All of this kind of lore was passed on from generation to generation in the *tithe airneáin*—houses where people went on night visits to yarn and tell stories. In these houses the ancestral memories were kept alive and transmitted to a younger generation. Nowadays we don't have *tithe airneáin*. The ascendancy of television ended that tradition and with it went all of the talk of genealogy and the lore of place.

Nothing remains of that house, the house of our origins in Mín 'a Leá, except a window which is incorporated into the stone wall around a field below Aindí Jimmy Sheáin's house. Anyway, that window is still there — a gaping hole in the wall, an opening to the past and perhaps to the future. As a community, it is important for us to contemplate that window so that we can achieve in the here and now a balance and an equilibrium between what is past and what is to come. Through that window we can try to engage the past and to envisage the future.

Like this one, the older houses were built in sheltered nooks in the land. They belonged, unobtrusively, with their surroundings. Nowadays our houses are statements of superiority, perched boldly in prominent positions dominating the landscape, breaking its natural contours. Too often these obtrusive buildings are habitations to house the ego rather than home.

Teach na Míne is a roofless stone dwelling in the bog overlooking Loch an Ghainimh. It was used as a *céilí* house, a place where locals gathered to have a hooley after a hard day's work, particularly after a *meitheal*. The *meitheal* was the name given to a working party when the neighbours banded together as a workforce to help a needy family or an elderly or ailing neighbour with turf-cutting or harvesting potato-digging or hay-making or whatever seasonal chore that needed to be done.

When they finished a day's work they would have an *oíche go maidin* — night until morning of dancing and merry-making. What a wonderful night spot to hang out in! A moon like a spotlight above Errigal, a shimmer of stars on the lake, a romantic expanse of bog all around. It's a place for a grand passion. Sometimes I do my own solo dance at Teach na Míne, a stomp and a prance to the thrill of a skylark.

My ancestral house, the original abode of my people when they settled in Mín 'a Leá five generations ago was, until recently, a tumbledown ruin but Ian Joyce, a distinguished artist who has come to live in my townland has restored this derelict house and kept its essential character and charm.

My people abandoned it sometime in the 1880s and moved to another site, a stone's throw away but lower down in Mín 'a Leá — the house where I was reared. According to family lore my people abandoned their old house when a man drowned in Loch an Ghainimh, the nearby lake. *D'éirigh siad uaigneach*, they became lonely as a result of this tragic drowning. But loneliness is not an exact equivalent of *uaigneas*. Loneliness implies an absence of people in your life, being bereft of company. Of course you can feel this aloneness, this lonesomeness acutely in the midst of a crowd if somehow you feel apart from it. But *uaigneas* in Irish is another matter entirely. It's a feeling of having stepped across the threshold of the Other-world. A creepy, chilling fear enters into you, inhabits you, possesses you. An eerie energy takes shape within you. The hair rises on your head. You break out in a cold sweat. That's *uaigneas*. It's spooky and strange. *Uaigneas* I think, presupposes, that there are many realms of being, all co-existent. Sometimes, inadvertently, we broach one of these domains—be it the Otherworld of the *Sidhe* or the ghostly Realm of the Dead. Then the strange spookiness comes over you, intensely and uncannily. That's what my great-grandfather's family experienced and they fled the house.

So many derelict houses draped in wild ivy; so many ruins strangled by scrub hazels; so many meadows abandoned to heather; so many fields where potatoes and corn were grown, now taken over by tenacious crops of rushes and brambles. The seasonal calendar of farm routines is no longer a concern in theses wiped-out communities. The reality now is that the cartwheel and the plough, the harrow and the sickle are installed in front of hillside holiday-homes to create a rural ambience.

Here I walk the hills, particularly at twilight, *"idir an dá sholas,"* as we say, a time where the snipe like a kid goat bleats in the darkening air and the grouse with its husky cackle flits across the wild bogs. This is also a walking meditation, a time of reflection, a tracing of past lives, and a longing to belong to what is gone; a yearning to bring the past into the present so that it will have a future. On these walks I delve into the living sod of my memory and feel, sometimes, as if in a vision the lives of my forbears taking shape in front of me, unearthing themselves, perhaps, out of the depths of my own racial memory.

'The Deserted Townlands'/ 'Na Bailte Bánaithe' is a poem in which I attempt to bring this notion to light.

THE DESERTED VILLAGES

1

At evening, in the half-light,
I see them taking shape
out of the mist that veils the dead.

My grandfather, my people's
people, I see them
working out in the open.

The men reaping in fields
that aren't there anymore,
The women milking cows

In a sunny cattle-fold,
the children playing hide and seek
among stooks and sheaves.

As far as my eyes can see,
the dead, teeming with life,
are gathering on the old sod.

In the small deserted villages
of the foothills, in Mín na bPoll,
in Prochlais, in Mín na gCopóg.

From the Mín of my vision
they come, those buried generations
walking steadily along,

looking as though they miss
their old haunts, these villages
where they spent their days.

Now wending their way
homewards, their footsteps as quiet
as the night closing in.

4

Bound to what is unspoken,
they carry a grave wisdom, silently,
between the living and the dead.

They are immured in silence now,
the toilers, the hummock breakers
of Mín na bPoll, of Prochlais, of Mín na gCopóg.

Wordless now the once mighty Sweeneys,
the Harkins, noted for their lore,
and the O'Boyles, beloved for their beauty.

There's a keening moan on the wind
that's coming west from Altán
while here a spider spins

A death shroud in the gapped
window of the old house
where long ago my people lived.

On Ard na mBothóg as fog
draws down its blackout blinds
on Mín na bPoll, on Prochlais,

On Mín na gCopóg, I stand alone.
Each ruin is interred in silence
and no word or rune will unlock a stone.

—*excerpts translated by the author*

2. Poetry matters

In a State of Flux—Irish Poetry 1980–89

> *Words can't defeat Evil but they*
> *can help us cope better with it*
>
> —*Franz Kafka*

In a world severely threatened, now more than ever, with unrestrained violence and relentless terrorism; ethnic strife and bloodshed; ruthless tyrannies and oppressed multitudes; large scale starvation and gratuitous destruction of our environment, poetry sounds pointless. In these scary circumstances the word 'poetry' sounds shallow and a sham. But that's only if we cling stubbornly to the snappy belief that poetry is the reserve of the Academe—a highbrow curiosity, obscure and worthless—but not if poetry is seen as a crucial medium of change, as a vital and an eloquent instigator of meaning within society as a whole. And I stress meaning because mankind requires meaning—or at least a search for meaning—and poetry when it embodies its true calling is a quest for meaning, for truth. Poetry at its best affirms lasting human values. It confronts oppression. It opposes repression. Poems are always on the side of light, always on the side of life. There is no higher religion, according to the great Bengali poet, R. Tagore, than sympathy for all that lives. Poetry, therefore, cannot and should not represent any collectivity or any superimposed set of values; the poet by defending his/her personal rights and independence is also defending every individual's rights and ondependence. The American poet Charles Olson's observations about filling our given space is, I think, a pertinent statement in this respect:

> . . . a man; carved
> out of himself, so wrought he
> watching the river flow
> fills his given space, makes
> traceries sufficient to
> others' needs . . .
> here is
> social action, for the poet
> anyway, his
> politics, his
> needs . . .

"To make traceries sufficient to others' needs," as Olson endorses in his poem is, I think, an exemplary and effective role for the poet. In the profoundest sense it means to be politically aware. In these terrible times when man's inhumanity to man has grown to grotesque proportions, we all, poets included, must revere ourselves, recognise ourselves as life that wants to live among other forms of life that want to live. And isn't that what compassion is all about—an imaginative recognition of and a humane understanding towards all life forms. In these dehumanising days poetry needs to be compassionate, needs to care.

Faced by incoherence and chaos, by conspiracies against dignity and justice, poets have to summon a greater faith in human compassion than ever before, a stronger belief in human endurance to affirm love, to endorse truth. My choice of ten poems exemplifies and expresses that belief. These poems, I believe, want to establish a redemptive, humane perspective in a world where such perceptions seems to have been blurred. These poems embody a heady mix of aesthetic complexity and social commitment, a new daring to address and challenge settled habits of style and an irrepressible boldness to defy stultifying social conventions. All of these poems pursue a genuine search for fresh meanings and methods, for authentic moments of faith and hope, for certain dependable continuities. They are concerned not only with the meaning of life but also with the life of meaning. They are about states of soul as much as they are about states of society.

With their risky utterance and their urgency they are liberating rather than limiting:

1. Paul Durcan, 'The Haulier's Wife Meets Jesus on the Road Near Moone'.
2. Seamus Heaney, 'Terminus'.
3. Ciaran Carson, 'Dresden'.
4. Nuala Ní Dhomhnaill, 'An bhábóg bhriste'.
5. Michael Davitt, 'Do Pound, ó Dhia'.
6. Gréagóir Ó Dúill, 'Dubhghall'.
7. Gabriel Rosenstock, 'Chuig mo Chéile atá ag Sclábhaíocht ar an mBalla Mór'.
8. Thomas McCarthy, 'The Non-aligned Storyteller'.
9. Francis Harvey, 'The Deaf Woman in the Glen'.
10. Eamon Grennan, 'Four Deer'.

Something of the spirit of the decade is, I hope, revealed in these poems. In the 80s Irish society was confused by social changes. There was a distinct rift —albeit a hesitant, ambivalent one—between church and state. The crozier no longer held sway in the Dáil, no longer transfixed the domestic. Assumptions that were once fixed and familiar were in an alarming state of flux. We were bewildered by the Kerry Babies scandal, shocked by the Ann Lovett tragedy, stunned by the Hunger Strikes. The economic slump depressed us. The exodus of our young unsettled us. Ireland of the 80s was more a state of absence than a place of presence. It was a void that was occasionally filled and enlivened by the holy commotion of the Moving Statues, by the spirited displays of the Soccer Squad, by the wild jolt of energy that was U2.

Trapped in their own helplessness, poets like everybody else, can also develop an emotional and aesthetic fatigue. However, I think, that the ten poets represented here, responded to life in the Ireland of the 80s with creative eagerness and exuberance. They overcame the small-mindedness and the sordidness of the present by putting the immediate into a broader historical or mythical perspective. They seek shapes and figures, archetypal patterns that will allow them to confirm and clarify their own human experience, however tenuously, against a more resonant backdrop. Accustomed to discontinuities and discordances, to ironies of identity, to self-doubt, some of them attempt to shift to a distant objective correlative the more pressing concerns of their poetry so that the aesthetic and ethical burdens of their lives will become a little bit more bearable, a little bit more understandable. They became adept at appropriating the irregular rhythms of life in the society around them to the private pressures of the psyche. They are "non-aligned storytellers" with an impulse toward the parable rather than the polemic.

All of these poets are familiar with the scathing tact and the dazzling shifts of subterfuge practised by the East European poets of the 60s and 70s. Under the hydra-headed monster of totalitarianism with its creepy censorship, Zbigniew Herbert in Poland, Miroslav Holub in Czechoslovakia, Vasko Popa in Yugoslavia, Marin Sorescu in Romania, all became connoisseurs of cogent irony, virtuosos of outspoken obliquities and well-versed masters of poetic double-talk. They astounded all of us who encountered them, even in translation, with the tightrope artistry of their poetries. In the face of ideological tyrannies and political correctness these poets carried a weighty moral sensibility, a deeply committed defence of humane values in times that enforced the depersonalisation of man.

The poets included here deploy some of the imaginative dexterity and the narrative cunning of these East European poets in their own handling of violent histories and deceitful politics. Heaney, Ó Dúill, McCarthy, Rosenstock, Carson, all draw upon historical anecdotes, potted histories and anecdotal personae that correspond somehow to their own politically embattled situations. Within their own experiences, their own emphases, they all bear witness to the tumult of our times. They are conscious of the fact that they inhabit history, that their various destinies are played out under its fierce eye; that their personal and particular histories coincide with a much broader history. Therefore, they are alert as an antenna to its signals. In Heaney's marvellous 'Terminus'—an eloquent and an enduring achievement, written it seems in response to the post hunger strike stalemate—there is an austere amplitude. It is a poem that broadens the specific by giving it a mythical source and an epic scope, that is pitched beautifully between public utterance and private testimony. It is a poem about boundaries and borders, about tribal and political entrapment, about factions and frictions. But despite the disabling embitterments that bind it, it seems to me to be a poem that strives for or at least implies boundlessness. The ten poems I have selected represent man's spirit coming to terms with the anguish of being. They all aspire, either openly or covertly, to the redemptive and affirmative condition of boundlessness.

I would like to cast a cursory eye over the poetic careers of these ten poets during the 80s. That decade gave us the taut and elegant poems of Frank Harvey, a sadly neglected poet. Elegiac and lyric, regional and specific, true to their own world, they also open out wholeheartedly to other worlds. With their loops and links and whorls of sound, they vibrate in the memory with a profoundly mantric quality. The reinvented Ciaran Carson came forth in the 80s with his exquisitely fabricated, daringly digressive, thickly textured innovations and we witnessed the Irish lyric being opened up to more challenging and arresting modes of perceptions and reflections than it had ever attempted before.

We have the keenly perceptive chronicles of Thomas McCarthy, in which the thwarted ideals and misplaced hopes of the new Irish Republic are scrutinized and exposed in the hope, I assume, that some of this burdensome inheritance can be abandoned. Then, and only then, can we shape up to new responsibilities, new futures. Eamon Grennan gave us his rapt contemplations of the commonplace, active meditations that ease us into alertness. We have in Eamon Grennan a true Seer, somebody who reveals the world anew. Reading his poems, we become more eye, more ear, more conscious of the momentousness of the ordinary. As a groundbreaking literary transgressor, Paul Durcan has been much lauded but much more castigated. But I hark back to Swift, *"When a true genius appears you will know him by this sign, all the dunces are in a confederacy against him."* In the 80s Durcan moved into an intensely creative spell. His best poems are savagely witty, heartbreakingly accurate documentaries of the changing social and sexual mores of the Ireland of our times. Dramatic monologues—erotic, irreverent, delirious—that stomp and frolic between pastoral romance and full-frontal frankness. With the depth and intelligence of their insights, the integral and absolute humanity of their vision, these are poems to be cherished, to be revered, even. Nuala Ní Dhomhnaill, one of the essential voices of our times, came to prominence in the 80s. She is a poet with a world appeal and a world relevance. As we set forth on our voyage into the unknown millennium we need the visionary sorcery of her poems—the talismanic power of their revelations to steer us into safe havens, to light up our mortal days and nights. She is a poet of love, a loving poet. Her love extends to every blooming thing. Fauna and flora abound and bloom in her poems. Without this love, as Gary Snyder pointed out (and rightly so), we can end, even without war, with an uninhabitable planet. Her work is another splendid sample of what Máire Mhac an tSaoi characterised as *"a living literature in a fast dying minority language."*

Here, in her work and in the work of her gifted contemporaries, we hear the triumphant whoop of a threatened language which—despite the gloom and doom—is in these poems, alive to all the demands and the challenges of our century. Michael Davitt, a liberating force in Irish language poetry, published his Selected Poems in the late 80s. The jazzy urgency of his style made Irish go bebop in the night with a swinging, snazzy self-confidence. For a lot of us who came to poetry in the 70s and 80s he was the tuned-in, amped-up, street-wise cosmopolitan who set the fads, the lingo and the stances. His is an eloquent achievement, a record of richly human poems brought back from the edge of the abyss, from a zone of fear and desperation. Poems that make a tender appeal to the heart as they attempt to make sense of the world's grief and the soul's despair. In Gréagóir Ó Dúill's poems of the 80s, the instability of the self and the perishability of man amidst the upheavals of history is evoked with a fierce individualistic expressiveness. If Ó Dúill occasionally uses incongruities of expression or a more discordant diction it is because the existing resources of language become inadequate to his needs and he has to speak as an initiator, as an instigator of language. In this world of turmoil and transience, the poem, carved out with extreme difficulty, becomes a small illuminated moment of stability and truth. Gabriel Rosenstock's frame of reference is broader than that of any other poet writing in the Irish language at present. A poet who has assimilated much of what is best in world poetry, the range of his inventiveness is limitless. In the 80s he made wonder-voyages into Oriental realms of the imagination in search of emotional correlatives — plausible parallels from a remote historical past — that would allow him to make sense of the malaise of the present.

The four Irish language poems presented here are accompanied by translations. Gabriel Rosenstock, our greatest traveller across linguistic and cultural borders, said that translation was like a blood transfusion between friends. Frank Sewell, the most gifted poet of a new generation of Northern Ireland poets stated that the translator goes down on history; a cunning linguist. In this country, English and Irish have been colliding with each other for centuries; both physically and psychically. English poetry, I think, has benefited from and has been enriched by these encounters. Clarke, Kavanagh, Heaney, Montague, Muldoon, Carson, Meehan have all taken sustenance from the expressive energies of Irish. The ghost, the spectre of Irish, is continuously making an appearance in English-language poetry in this country. It's like a poltergeist, upsetting the furniture of the poem, shuffling with the syntax, breathing through the metrics, uttering its own strange sounds. It's now time, I think, for Irish-language verse to benefit from the scope and the range of English. I am delighted with the way that Frank Sewell has managed to invoke my own poems in English. He has found a voice and a register for them that seems to me to be acceptable in English. Likewise, Paul Muldoon and John Montague in particular, by deft and clever handling of tone and texture, have succeeded in making the poems of Michael Davitt and Nuala Ní Dhomhnaill speak in poetry and not in translationese. It just goes to prove, as somebody said, that poetry has many tongues but a single language.

Selecting ten poems to represent the decade is outrageously stingy. It's like trying to bake a cake using ingredients of only one syllable. Another ten would be equally niggardly but here they are, if only for the record: Derek Mahon's 'Ovid in Tomis'; Liam Ó Muirthile's 'An Parlús'; Dermot Bolger's 'Snuff Movies'; Michael O'Loughlin's 'Latin as a Foreign Tongue'; Paul Muldoon's 'The Sightseers'; Áine Ní Ghlinn's 'Gealt'; James Simmons's 'From the Irish'; Medbh McGuckian's 'Slips'; Biddy Jenkinson's 'Cáitheadh'; Eavan Boland's 'The Glass King'.

The flow goes on, a ripple in the rockpools here, a cascading torrent there. Sometimes breaking its banks, extending its limits; at other times languishing in backwaters. But always an outward flow, out to the ocean, unbounded. I will end with a Maori poem:

> From the family of mountains
> to the endless sea;
> I am the River
> the River is me.

Micheál Ó Conghaile

Micheál Ó Conghaile is a latter-day Connemara surrealist, a spinner of dark extravagant fables. In his short stories he has created his own fabulous terrestrial domain, a mythical realm both intimate and cosmic where psychodrama meets magical realism. These stories with their marvelous mix of horseplay and high seriousness could have been written by Harpo Marx and Hieronymus Bosch in a shebeen in Muiceanach-Idir-Dhá-Sháile. And I'm sure Scheherazade would have told the Caliph these sort of stories if instead of being born in Baghdad, she had come from Barna.

'Ar Pinsean sa Leithreas' (In Retirement in the Loo) is one of these marvelously fabricated parables. It is the bizarre story of a man who locks himself away in the lavatory believing that no one dies there. And I'm inclined to agree with him. This is evident to all of us who listen to the local news on Radio na Gaeltachta. You'd never hear this kind of death notice: "*Johnny Connelly died peacefully this morning in the toilet of his County Council bungalow at Sraith Salach.*" It would be socially acceptable for him to die in his bedroom or out on the bog or even, out on the tear but not in the lavatory. It was widely aired that Elvis Presley died in his privy after eating a tin of sardines, but that was in America.

The narrator in the loo by insulating himself from clocks and calendars, deadlines and duties, moons, tides and changes believes that he will live forever. The dialogue with the priest and the lawyer who comes to put his worldly and spiritual affairs in order is both a standoff and a shit-hot exchange of irreverence. Ó Conghaile sustains this wacky narrative with a deadpan authority and ends it with a master stroke dénouement.

Another of his stories, 'Seacht gCéad Uaireadóir' (Seven Hundred Watches) is set in a spooky little watch shop down a dead-end street. It's staffed by a grim looking, inscrutable old man who declines to sell any watches. He just keeps winding them, watch after watch. He is the custodian of time, he says, overseeing its pulse and flow, and although all time is within his brief he himself lives a clockwork existence passing the time by keeping his hands busy.

It's a typical offbeat Ó Conghaile story where the customary and the familiar are undermined by a dreamed-up zany logic that is at odds with all predictable reasoning. Ó Conghaile is interested, I think, not so much in Truth but what ought to be Truth.

In his stories our fleeting dream life takes shape in vivid and memorable details. Like Kafka, Borges, Marques, the familiar is fabulized and the improbable is habitualized.

His novel *Sna Fir* is a defining moment in coming out literature in Irish. The need to write oneself into existence is at the heart of this eloquent, exploratory novel. It is a savagely witty, piercingly accurate story of a young Connemara man's tough passage out of the closet. It is the first novel to exult and delight in the gay in Gaylic. But it's not only gay writing it is also great writing. It is a stunning evocation of changing social and sexual mores in the West of Ireland. A Connemara Homofesto.

In the world of Irish language letters Micheál Ó Conghaile occupies a position of eminence as a publisher. His remarkable press, Cló Iar-Chonnacht is now well known nationally and internationally. He has published the most daring of new voices and the most compelling of the established writers. To read his list of authors is to know where Irish language literature comes from and to see where it's going as it whoops and wheels its way into the future.

Burns: A Poet of Breath
for Murray Learmont

The life of Robert Burns (1759–96) is a life that was lived with passion and intensity. We can marvel at his exuberance of spirit, his impetuous impulses, his lofty inspiration. It is also a life saddened and certainly shortened by severe labour, chronic ill health and misery. And despite the loves and joys that he so keenly tasted he had ample proof from his own life "that man was made to mourn". And although he wept and mourned he also sang and rejoiced:

> Gie me ae spark o' Nature's fire,
> That's a' the learning I desire;
> Then tho' I drudge thro' dub an' mire
> At pleugh or cart,
> My muse, tho' hamely in attire,
> May touch the heart.

From 'Epistle to J. Lapraik, An Old Scottish Bard',
April 1, 1785

His moral constitution was much condemned by his Victorian biographers. They were outraged by his passions and excesses, his womanizing, his daring erotic anarchy. He relished the gift of life and sowed his wild oats abundantly amongst the fair sex of Ayrshire. If they had the latitude he fondly gave them his longitude. Most of his adult life he was beset by this mesh, this gridlock of sensuality.

He fathered 15 children, nine in lawful wedlock and six love children, the result of brief flings with various servant girls. These girls were dismissed by a friend of the poet's at the time as "burnished butterflies amusing his noontime leisure."

I don't think the #MeToo movement would take too kindly to that rash judgement and they would be right. But we live in a different time, a different place, with vastly different codes of behavior. Robbie gave these young over-trusting country girls his roving admiration if not his lasting attention.

Whatever about his loose morals and intemperate habits, Robbie Burns was, by all accounts, an expansive and generous spirit; a man gifted with an affectionate, compassionate, humane nature. He was a humanitarian. His sympathies were with the poor and the downtrodden; the oppressed, voiceless multitudes who suffered in silence. He hated the arrogance of privilege and in a justly famous poem 'A Man's a Man for a' That' proclaimed a brother-hood of universal charity:

That Man to Man, the world o'er
Shall brothers be for a' that

His empathy extended to the animal kingdom, to the mouse, the faithful old mare, the wounded hare, the dying sheep, the uprooted daisy. He was against animal cruelty and advocated in his poems on their behalf:

I'm truly sorry man's dominion,
Has broken nature's social union,
An' justifies that ill opinion,
Which makes thee startle
At me, thy poor, earth-born companion,
An' fellow-mortal!

This reverence for one of nature's lowly dwellers, this recognition of the mouse as a fellow creature and co-habitant of earth, sharing in the same life force as the poet sounded a note of visionary empathy that pre-dated Wordsworth and the Romantics and contributed, I'm sure, to the high and holy serious-ness in which they express their spiritual relationship with nature.

Burns had an ambivalent view of religion. 'No Churchman am I' is an early poem of his. In his correspondence he writes about religion as *the trick of the crafty few to lead the undiscerning many.*" And in another letter he declares *"But of all nonsense religious nonsense is the most nonsensical."*

He disliked the severe dogmas of Scottish Calvinism, its inflexible austerities and its heresy hunters; a creed that made a ceremony of death out of the miracle of life. He had no time for the hypocrisy, the rigidly self-righteous, the fanaticism and cant of much of the religious creeds that flourished around him. And he didn't conceal his disapproval "from such conceptions of my Creator, good Lord, deliver me." And in that marvelous poem 'To a Louse' he voices his contempt of false piety and posturing:

> O wad some Power the giftie gie us
> To see oursels as ithers see us!
> It wad frae mony a blunder free us,
> An' foolish notion:
> What airs in dress an' gait wad lea'e us,
> An' ev'n devotion!

I think that his own code of beliefs leaned more towards the notion of God as love — a love universally diffused and animating all of Creation, *"The light that led astray"* was still, he believed, a *"light from Heaven."*

Love was, of course, the great pervading passion of his life and likewise in his poetry Burns embraces all humanity.

The Unco Guid, the Holy Willies, the Hornbooks, the Saturday Night Cotters, the Man Made to Mourn, the tipsy Tam o'Shanter, the Mouse and the Louse . . . these poems are deeply-rooted chronicles of a particular time and place, but they are not exclusive to 18th century Ayrshire. They are universal and timeless and relevant to the here and now as much as they were to the then and there. That's why we are still engaged with them centuries later.

Burns and his family led a somewhat peripatetic lifestyle as tenant farmers, moving from one farm to another in the hope of improving their lot.

In 1766 they moved from their humble cottage in Alloway, (where Robbie was born in 1759) to a small farm, Mount Oliphant, two miles away.

11 years later in 1777 they left Mount Oliphant for a bigger farm at Lochlea, north of Ayr.
In 1783 Robbie and his brother Gilbert moved to Mossgiel, a farm situated on a bare upland to the east of the village of Mauchline.

In 1788—Robbie himself took possession of Ellisland, a farm in the vicinity of Dumfries. In 1791 he gave up the lease of Ellisland and moved permanently into the town of Dumfries, where he died in 1796 at the age of 37. The family labored very hard but fared badly. Despite their industry and good intentions they failed mostly because of a lack of capital, to improve the impoverished farms they rented.

"We lived very poorly," Robbie said, looking back at his life at Lochlea, " . . . *the cheerless gloom of a hermit with the unceasing toil of a galley-slave . . ."*
He began to write poetry *"to find some kind of counter-*

poise" to the dull, unprofitable drudgery of farm labour.

Although exceedingly poor as tenant farmers the Burns family, nevertheless, was distinguished by a superiority of manners and a refinement of taste that set them apart from their neighbours. De Quincy, the English poet and author quipped; *"Lucifer was as proud as Burns."*

The father, William Burns who died at Lochlea in 1783, exhausted and worn out by hard labour and financial struggles was a stern, religious man who appreciated the value of a good education and literacy if only to study the Bible. He himself wrote a kind of Catechism in standard English; a dialogue between father and son that highlighted the chief religious tenets that he wished his family to understand and practice.

The mother, Agnes, was a storehouse of folk-song and ballads.

Burns is often presented as the Ploughman Poet, a kind of rough, untutored, rustic original. Far from it. By the age of 13 he was reading novelists like Henry Fielding and Tobias Smollet and the very polished English essayists, Pope, Addison, Steele and Swift. He was very fortunate that a young teacher called John Murdoch befriended the family and supplied Robert with books.

Robbie Burns was a young man alive in an era of major historical upheavals. It was a time of great social change, of radicalism and revolution that changed the course of human destiny. In 1776 we have the American Declaration of Independence. In 1789 the fall of the Bastille and the French Revolution. In that same year George Washington became the first president of the U.S.A.

It was the age when Equality, Liberty and Fraternity became major aspirations for large segments of the populace. Influential works were published, books that changed public thinking about freedom and man's place in society—groundbreaking volumes like Adam Smith's *Wealth of Nations* (1776); Rousseau's *Confessions* (1776), Paine's *Rights of Man* (1790).

Burns was alert, attuned and sensitive to the thinking and the politics of his time. His great egalitarian psalm of life, 'A Man's a Man for a' That' attests to his humanistic principles. Actually his political activities and agitation was nearly the undoing of him. He barely escaped being sent to Botany Bay for treason and sedition on account of his sympathy with the British Reform Movement, a radical front inspired by the French Revolution. He was saved by the intercession of well-placed friends.

It was while he was farming at Mossgiel in 1785 that he met Jean Armour, daughter of a master mason from the town of Mauchline. She became his wife —eventually and *"the moon in his sky"* as he says—

"but alas!" as a contemporary acquaintance of Burns says, "not altogether unattended by other sister planets." His rakish behavior led to his public humiliation in the Kirk where he was publicly upbraided by the minister and made to sit on the "cutty stool" in front of the congregation and be branded a fornicator. Later he made mockery of all that with vigorous vernacular energy in poems like 'Holy Willies Prayer' and 'Welcome to a Bastard Wean':

> Welcome! my bonie, sweet, wee dochter,
> Tho' ye come here a wee unsought for,
> And tho' your comin' I hae fought for,
> Baith kirk and queir;
> Yet, by my faith, ye're no unwrought for,
> That I shall swear!

1786 was an important year in Burns' literary career. His first volume of poems was published in an edition of 600 copies and printed in Kilmarnock. *Poems, Chiefly in the Scottish Dialect*, was immediately acclaimed and *"the power of genius of this Heaven-taught ploughman"* was saluted by Henry MacKenzie, an influential author of that time.

The doors of Edinburgh's fashionable society were open to him and he mingled with the luminaries and the literati of the metropolis. The second edition of his poems appeared in Edinburgh in 1787—an enlarged edition with a print run of 2,800 copies at a price of 5 shillings. It was mostly financed by subscribers—the landed gentry and nobility, people like the Earl of Eglinton who took 40 copies, the Duchess of Gordon who took 21, and the Caledonian Hunt, they took 100.

In Edinburgh he met and had quite an amourous dalliance with Mrs Agnes MacLehose, "Clarinda," as he fondly called her, a veiled name to conceal their clandestine affair. She was a lively, cultivated, shapely lady, living a kind of widowhood in Edinburgh, her estranged husband being in the West Indies.

The correspondence between herself and Burns is fraught with her scruples of conscience about their affair and his all out desire for a *"bosom friendship"* and *"a consummation devoutly to be wished."* In a letter to her dated December 21, 1787 he says:

I don't know if you have any idea of my character but I wish you to see me as I am. I am, as most people of my trade are, a strange will o' the wisp being, the victim too frequently of much imprudence and many follies. My great constituent elements are pride and passion.

Her reply: *"Know you, I know you far better than you do me, like yourself I'm a bit of an enthusiast."*

In another letter she states, *"I am a strict Calvinist, one or two dark tenets excepted which I never meddle with"* and later she adds *"I often think I would have been a man but for some mistake of nature."*

Robbie in his letters pursues his epistolary seduction relentlessly:

I can easily enter into the sublime pleasures that your strong imagination and keen sensibility must derive from religion, particularly if a little in the shade of misfortune: but I own I cannot, without a marked grudge, see Heaven totally engross so amiable, so charming, a woman as my friend Clarinda; and should be very well pleased at a circumstance that would put it in the power of somebody (happy somebody!) to divide her attention, with all the delicacy and tenderness of an earthly attachment.

She must have given in to his hot-blooded pursuits and ardour. In her next letter she is much more laid back, so to say, more amenable to amour: "*I love you for your continued fondness, even after enjoyment; few of your sex have souls in such cases.*" And in a lovely letter dated January 9, 1788 she alikens the two of them "*You and I have some horse properties but more of the eagle and too much of the turtle dove.*"

Their affair continued until the end of 1791 but by then it seems that they had lost faith in their religion of the bosom. In one of his final letters to Clarinda he asks her for a favour—a girl called Jenny Clow who gave birth to a son of Burns in 1788 had fallen on hard times in Edinburgh and needed help—

I am sure she must have told you of a girl, Jenny Clow, who had the misfortune to make me a father (with contrition I own it) contrary to the laws of our most excellent constitution, in our holy Presbyterian hierarchy . . . can you send her five shillings in my name.

Unable to make a livelihood out of farming he entered the Excise Service as a common gauger at £50 annually in 1789. He had charge of ten parishes and rode on horseback about 200 miles a week discharging his duties among distillers of whiskey and publicans and keeping an eye on smugglers.

He was not in good health, suffering often from severe headaches, an irregular beat of the heart and rheumatic fever. Despite his misery, his ill health and his proneness to depression, he worked steadily with James Johnson and later with George Thomson on their major collections of Scottish song, rescuing from oblivion and neglect hundreds of songs and supplying new words to suit the melodies. More and more, poems gave way to song; a pouring forth of song that knew neither borders nor barriers. They came tumbling out of him in a cascade of sweetness — 'Ae Fond Kiss', 'My Love is Like' a Red Red Rose', 'Banks of Doon', 'Auld Lang Syne', 'Comin Throu the Rye', 'Scots Wha Hae', 'Sweet Afton', 'The Wild Mossy Mountains', 'Charlie He's My Darling' and hundreds of others, songs that are sung and cherished today the world over.

He died in poverty on the 21 July 1796. He was given a grandiose military funeral on the 25 July while his wife Jean Armour gave birth to his son Maxwell.

Whatever human faults and failures he had in his earthly life they are now buried with him in the grave—while his poems and songs live on gloriously — giving us a real carnival of colour, a liberating, libidinous jolt of joy to the spirit.

May the Karma of his genius continue to run over our nasty Dogmas.

Poet in Exile: The Poetry of Colette Ní Ghallchóir

It has taken a long time for women poets whether in Irish or in English to place themselves at the centre of Irish poetry. At the beginning of the twentieth century there were a number of compelling female poets, role models and foremothers: Katharine Tynan, Ethna Carbery, Emily Lawless, Eva Gore-Booth, Dora Sigerson Shorter, Susan Mitchell and, in Irish, Áine Ní Fhoghlú from Gaeltacht na Rinne and Úna Ní Fhaircheallaigh (Agnes O'Farrelly) from County Cavan. From the 1950s onwards they were discredited and mostly edited out of the canon. It was common, as Eavan Boland rightly points out, to shove women poets to the margins, to relegate and exclude them. Virginia Woolf once remarked that for most of history 'anonymous' was a woman.

Women were required to be accomplished in the domestic arts and to be capable child-bearers. They were to remain unselfishly subordinate, skilfully occupying the home domain but silent and invisible to the public sphere. They were not expected to be assertive or creative or a threat to any of the areas and disciplines traditionally dominated by men. They were much maligned by male commentators who depicted them as either sirens or shameless harlots, or else, conveniently lauded them as virtuous maidens and domestic goddesses. Fortunately, at least in the western world, more liberating times and the commitment of the feminist campaign has changed these perceptions and eased, somewhat, the severe constraints that silenced female creativity.

Now the female voice is at the heart of what is happening in Irish poetry both in Irish and in English. The unfettered, instinctual, free spirit of the female is coming to the fore. Women poets are writing the Irish poem from a whole different psychic experience, from the five senses, from the four elements, from the seven deadly sins and, of course, from their own lovely wiles of allurement.

Máire Mhac an tSaoi, a daring diva of delight, is crucial to that change. She has had a major say in the reshaping of the Irish poem. Her debut collection, *Margadh na Saoire*, published by Sáirséal & Dill in 1956—and largely ignored at the time by our English-speaking literati—is an extraordinary achievement, a landmark in the history of poetry in this country. Intense and intimate, emotionally courageous, skillfully crafted, lucid and luminous, it is by far the single most important volume of verse published by any woman up to that time in Ireland. She has been a mentor, a mother, a role model to a whole new generation of challenging voices, male and female, who have been empowered by her liberating aesthetic. As a sign of admiration and approval she has translated two of Colette Ní Ghallchóir's most significant poems.

"*Religion is for people who believe in hell; spirituality is for people who've been there*". They are the wise words of David Bowie, a man who has himself plummeted the depths but fatefully rose out of the dark gifted with song. Reading Colette Ní Ghallchóir's poems I get a sense that many of them come from a place of affliction. But, somehow, they have been redeemed and purified.

Her early upbringing was within sight of the Bluestack Mountains, an Irish-speaking area in the Donegal uplands famous for its storytellers and fiddlers. A lot of her early childhood was spent in her grandmother's house in the Glen of Glenties, a house noted for its music and its open door hospitality. Journeymen musicians like Johnny Doherty, the virtuoso tinsmith fiddler, often visited and played on his occasional round of the Glen. For Colette that was a place of grace, a dominion of homely domesticity guided by her grandmother. Her beloved Glen was a green-wooded nook of wonder.

However her childhood contentment was abruptly disrupted when her parents decided to leave this lovely sheltered glen and move to Gaoth Dobhair, her father's native place, forty miles away; a stony coastal area exposed to harsh Atlantic winds. This bleak, treeless landscape unsettled her and left her grieving for her lost glen. The creative touch, it seems to me, empowered Colette to endure, to leave her anguish behind and to refocus her mind and her energies. Distilled out of that ferment of grief she made poems that are meaningful and uplifting. The walking wounded are the ones who give the most acute account of what it means to be truly alive.

Elegiac and grave, these poems shun any sort of high-pitched shrill of suffering in favour of a more subdued ordinariness of speech. Her artistry as a poet is embodied in that austerity. Imbued with a natural simplicity that seems at times elemental, these poems speak with the dazzle of raindrops trickling from the blackthorns of Gleann Mór on a spring morning. They are sibilant and fluent as a tongue of water murmuring among the stones of Abhainn Fhia:

DIÚLTÚ

Ní thig leo mé a chloí,
ní thig.
Brisfidh mé amach
mar fhéar ar thuí,
mar bhiolar ag fás ar chlasán,
nó, dála an ghabhair bhradaigh,
íosfaidh mé an féar glas
ar bharr na Screige go fóill.

REFUSAL

They will not stop me,
no.
I will break out
as grass grows
on thatch,
or cress
on a brook.
The day will come
when the greedy goat
will eat
the green grass on
top of Screig.

—translated by Nuala Ní Dhomhnaill

I'm struck by the verbal precision of her poems, their ability to be plain without being prosaic. She knows when to enrich the language of a poem and when to economize. In a lovely poem by the great American poet, Ted Deppe, he evokes Wittgenstein out in the wilds of Connemara talking to the crows and urging them: "Look very closely before you think and, only then, if ever, speak!" That is Colette Ní Ghallchóir's modus operandi. When she speaks it is with great compression charged with a vivid fusion of word and image. An insight begot in silence and brought forth with clarity:

SMÉARA

Nuair a fheicim
sméara dubha ag lobhadh
ar na dreasógaí tráthnóna fómhair,

nó an sneachta ag cascairt,
'na dheoir agus 'na dheoir,
ar Thaobh an Leithid,
sílim gur ceart
géilleadh don ghrá i gcónaí,
is cuma cén áit, cén t-am, nó cén uair.

BERRIES

When I see
blackberries withering
on autumn afternoon brambles,
or the snow disperse,
drop by drop,
on Taobh an Leithid,
I believe one should
always surrender to love,
no matter where, or when the hour.

—translated by Áine Durcan

Colette is very responsible in her duty to language
and careful about its integrity. I admire that. Denise
Levertov stated somewhere that poets having
language in their custody must recognize it as
another form of life, a common resource to be
cherished and cared for in the same way that we
should show a responsible concern for the earth and
its waters and its teeming life forms. She berated
those would-be poets who are irresponsible in their
duty to language, irreverent about its dignity and
careless about its integrity. This kind of poet, she
said, is contributing effectively to the erosion of
language just as the greedy farmer impoverishes the
soil or the grabbing industrialist pollutes the rivers.

Colette Ní Ghallchóir believes firmly that it is her sacred duty to safeguard language; to prevent it from becoming debased and diminished. She wants to augment it, not deplete it. She knows full well that the task is even greater for a poet like herself writing in a threatened minority language. Urgency and accuracy is needed to rescue and to reclaim. In 'Mo Chóta', for example, which can be taken as a correlative for Irish—she gives it back its ancestral dignity by praising its expressive strengths and its guttural warmth.

As regards tradition Colette strives for a vigorous continuity between the past and the present. She allies folksong with new forms; she couples native fluency with a modern idiom. Exile, loss and a yearning for the beloved Gleann Mór of her early childhood is a theme that throbs like a raw nerve in her poems. Her family moved from An Gleann Mór to Gaoth Dobhair, a short distance spatially but for the child it was overwhelming. She was uprooted from all that she knew and loved in a stable world and thrown headlong into a far-off, alien community. She has written poignantly about the loss of that edenic past and her longing to regain it even if it is in death:

FAOI NA FÓDA

Nuair a chuirfidh sibh mise
sa ghainimh mhín sin,
ní chloisfidh mise
fuaim an aigéin mhóir
ag lapadáil fá Ghabhla,

ach glór binn an Abhainn Fhia
ag crónán sa Ghleann.

UNDER THE SOD

When you bury me
in the fine sand,
I will not hear
the noise of the great ocean
lapping by Gabhla,
but the sweet sound
of the Owenea
murmuring in the Glen.

—*translated by Nuala Ní Dhomhnaill*

These poems 'An tAmharc Deireannach', 'Spiorad mo Chine', 'An Gleann Mór', although localised in their focus, have a universal appeal. They speak to everyone who has suffered the ache of separation and the anguish of exile. These poems and others like them—variations on the theme of exile—give us rare insights into the condition of displacement. Exile is a land off nostalgia where you fret about your home place in case it changes. That can be risky for the poet. Colette avoids any mawkishness about the past and yet writes poems that are emotionally demanding and heart-stunningly moving.

"*You can't change the past,*" as Carlo Gébler says in *Father and I*, a memoir that maps out and shapes his failed relationship with his father, "*but with understanding you can sometimes draw the poison out of it.*" That's what Colette did in her poetry. She has, somehow, managed to summon up a belief and a faith in the human heart to establish a dependable perspective in a world where perspective is adrift or missing:

SAILEOG

Nuair atá an ghaoth láidir
lúbaim
cromann mo cheann
ar mo chosa
gidh gur tréan an ghaoth
ní bhrisim
nó níor bhris
go n-uige seo.

WILLOW

When the wind blows
I bend down
I stoop so low
my head down to my toes
though the four winds blow
I do not break
unbroken, undaunted,
until now.

—*translated by Máire Wren*

Although the backdrop to some of the poems is relentlessly bleak, the work itself is redeeming for it represents the spirit coming to terms with suffering.

In her poetry, Colette Ní Ghallchóir is also alert to the unjust realities of our society. There is a strong social engagement in these poems, a deeply committed stand against injustice and oppression. The un-flinchingly realistic account of the rape and the loss of innocence of an altar boy in 'Roghnaithe' conveys with brutal clarity this heinous crime. 'Ar an Lagán' tells the nightmarish story of a woman caught in an endless cycle of poverty, childbirth and futility. Be it the Donegal of the past or the Somalia of the present the entrapment of poverty is still with us. This poem reverberates with that terrible truth and in its integral humaneness stirs in the reader a sense of pity and perhaps, even a more compassionate empathy with suffering humanity. 'Antain' is one of Colette's most powerful and resonant poems, a tragic story about the vicissitudes of exile in a poem that is intense and dramatic and where her feelings are palpably tangible, she laments the death of a man whose life has come to nothing; someone bedevilled by a wretched fate and now as a final inequity gets a lonely desolate burial in a foreign place far from his people's graveyard by the sea. This poem has the "lyric cry" that Sorley MacLean so much admired in a poem. That means a rare felicity of expression, the enduring clarity of the right words. In this poem we hear the Irish language voicing itself into the light with a lyrical self-assurance that is both encouraging and gladdening.

I know from Colette herself that two writers from her area have left a lasting impression on her and shaped, in no small way, the thrust of her work.

Patrick McGill (1890–1963), one of Donegal's fore-most writers was born in the Glen of Glenties and from abject poverty rose to become a household name amongst the London glitterati. In a run of gritty novels—*Children of the Dead End* (1914) and *The Rat Pit* (1915) being the most popular—he depicted with unflinching realism the grim conditions of his people; their impoverishment, their discontent, their powerlessness. His most memorable characters are dispossessed, exiled outcasts, children of the dead end as he so aptly named these oppressed Irish immigrants. McGill's writing, because of its candid depiction of chronic alcoholism, violence and prostitution amongst the underprivileged Irish in Britain was condemned by a disapproving clergy at home who did not want to have such disquieting social issues aired in public. His courageous championing of 'the great oppressed' has always appealed to Colette's own sense of justice and her innate humanitarian instincts.

Colette is a great admirer of Madge Heron (1915–2002), a wonderfully wayward poet from Fintown, a high-minded socialist and a native feminist who distained clerical authority and could not live under such a harsh repressive code of beliefs and so left her home for a more liberating life in London. Her daring, her high-seriousness, her fight for human dignity are all traits that appeal to Colette and they have been for her a shaping force and a source of inspiration. 'Ar an Imeall', 'Tiomna', 'Clog an Phobail' and 'Mo Bhealach Féin' attest to her own sense of rage and frustration at the limiting conventions of her community but they also bear witness and affirm her invigorating independence. Madge Heron who died in penury in London and whose poetry is sadly neglected would, I'm sure, appreciate and admire the continuing struggle for social justice expressed in these poems.

Colette has written movingly about relationships but she is at her best when she reflects and puzzles over the thwarted intimacies of love.

AN FEAR UASAL

Sleamhnaíonn tú chugam anois,
ar thrá, tráthnóna samhraidh,
do lámha thar mo choim,
do shúile dubha ag stánadh,
lán den fhuacht folaithe
a bhí i ndán dom.

Níos moille
agus duilleoga
ag titim ar ár ngrá,
thit an litir scoir
go fuarchúiseach
tríd an chomhla.

THE GENTLEMAN

You drift slowly towards me now
on a shore at the ebb of a summer's day,
your hands around my waist,
your black eyes staring,
full of the concealed cold
that was to be my fate.
Later as the autumn leaves
were falling on our fervour,

your farewell letter
fell indifferently
from the letter box.

—*translated by Máire Wren*

An eloquent poem of mourning and memory. There are also poems like 'An Fear Mór' that hints at the darker, sinister, abusive side of relationships. In many of her poems she manages to compress large areas of human experience into short, succinct, sensitive insights. Sometimes they sparkle with a genuinely achieved wisdom:

STOCAÍ

Tá do ghrá
mar a bheadh stocaí olla,
te, tirim, anuas ar mo chorp,
ach, corruair, cuireann ribeacha
na holla tochas ionam.

STOCKINGS

Your love
is like woolly socks,
warm, dry next to my skin
but sometimes the ribbing
causes itching.

—*translated by Gabriel Rosenstock*

Colette is a well-versed epigrammatist. These self-effacing fragments have the power and the poignancy of haiku. Many of them are prompted by a mystical impulse and a daring sense of the numinous. They have the sublime ability to move us into wonder. *"They catch the heart off guard and blow it open"* is a line by Seamus Heaney that aptly catches the power of the poems.

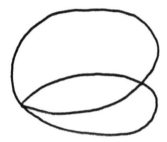

Burning Sage: The Poetry of Gabriel Rosenstock

Gabriel Rosenstock, our most prolific writer in the Irish language, is a vast subject matter, an expanding universe of words that keeps growing and growing.

Poet, dramatist, novelist, children's writer, essayist, editor, translator, encourager. I am dazzled by the huge and heady daring of his Work.

For more than forty years he has been a luminous and a liberating force in Irish literature. With his energy and enterprise, his stir and sparkle he has helped in no small way to liven up and embolden the arts in our country.

As a mentor he has energized many of us by his encouragement and counsel. He has the capacity to put other people in contact with their own creative vitality, to make them receptive to the inexhaustible cosmos of creativity within themselves, to make them voyagers in the universe of their own imaginations.

I first met Gabriel Stefan Rosenstock as he called himself in those days at Slógadh, the annual Gael-Linn youth extravaganza—which sadly is no more —in 1972. I had read his poems in the magazines; they were already causing a bit of commotion in the Irish language literary world, stirring up a somewhat stale scene. I was excited by their offbeat themes, their catchy wordplay, their brash uninhibited playfulness. Alive and vivid, they strutted right off the page and into my mind in a way that the pale and bookish poems of the classroom failed to do. This exotic presence with a name alien to Irish— which gave an added mystique to the poems— became my role model as I attempted my own first fledgling flights in poetry. For me, a brooding teenager in the throes of poetry, his poems were messages in a bottle from a distant Tír na nÓg; a revitalised, groovy Gaelic Ireland that flourished defiant and free on the margins of English.

Meeting him at that festival was a momentous occasion for me. He had judged the poetry competition and awarded me the main prize. I was fired up at the prospects of meeting him. And I was not let down as happens so often with hero worship. Here was this commanding presence, eloquent, perceptive, engaging and, best of all, responding to my poems with delight and affection. Listening to him on that glorious April afternoon in 1972, a new door was blown open for me onto poetry; a liberating doorway.

He advised me that poetry is more about divination than data; more about feelings than facts. It was not so much Truth he was seeking in poetry but what ought to be Truth. He was urging me to think of poems as lived experiences and not as thought-up experiences. Poetry as perceptions of the heart was what he wanted and not as conceptions of the mind.

I sensed in him a joyous creativity, an abounding curiosity about life, a need to bite into and taste the multitudinous and teeming flavours of the world and the Word. He stressed that poetry lifts us out of spiritual torpor and leads us into a richly sensual, ecstatic even, sense of the Divine; well beyond the constraints of doctrinaire religions.

An impressionable youth, I was enthralled by the beauty and sublimity of his ideas. And like a conjuror drawing doves out of a hat of abundance, he let a flock of those bright ideas loose in my imagination.

Gabriel is a child of the Sixties and together with his friend Michael Davitt (1950–2005), brought all of the expanded-mind exuberance of that decade to bear on the writing of poetry in the Irish language.

That sixties-state-of-mind —getting high on expan-siveness—primed their poetry and shaped the imaginative scope of it. As editors of *Innti*, their flamboyantly subversive poetry journal, and with the precocious brilliance of Nuala Ní Dhomhnaill and Liam Ó Muirthile, they made Irish get-up-and-go with dash and swagger.

In Gabriel's case the bliss business of Eastern beliefs gave his poetry a rich shimmering of mysticism. Blake and burning sage gave his poems an incandes-cent glow. Swami Vivekananda, Sri Aurobino, Krishnamurti, Ravi Shankar, Rajneesh, Suibhne Geilt, Æ. (George Russell) were some of his guardian an-gels; the spirit guides who enabled him to blend Vedic and Druidic strains into a rich sensuous, ecstatic melody; a new utterance in Irish.

***

A slow but formative period of modernism had set in ever since Pádraig Mac Piarais, (1879–1916) a genuine messenger of modernity, argued for a new aesthetic in Irish. In a handful of bleak and beautiful poems he conveyed human vulnerabilities and personal frailties in a startlingly modern manner. Liam Gógan (1891–1979) was another innovative influence; an erudite and intensely creative formalist with an ear to European trends, he explored new forms of expression to deal with the complexities of modern life and the disillusionments of a post-independence state. But it was not until the late 40s and early 50s when the great triumvirate of Ó Direáin, Ó Ríordáin and Máire Mhac an tSaoi met the challenges of their times with a new inventiveness in theme, language and tone that an identifiably Irish modernism emerged. Ó Ríordáin's (1916–1977) first volume, the magisterial *Eireaball Spideoige* (1952), is a majestic sweep of intense lyrics that dramatize his existential malaise with Baudelairean grandeur, a truly modern work in its delicate handling of unsettled identities within the dark and murk of the psyche.

Ó Direáin (1910–1988) and Máire Mhac an tSaoi (1922–) were not lagging behind in their efforts to attain contemporaneity. In a country desperately seeking to define itself, they were equally at pains to try to reconfigure an idiom that would pay homage to the sonorous native achievement in poetry but also move it into the daily expediencies of living speech. It is a testimony to their craft and ardour that they brought forth a poetry that resonates with a native lyricism and yet in form and thematic concerns embodies the harsh strength of a modern sensibility.

Throughout the Sixties, outstanding poets like Eoghan Ó Tuairisc (1919–1982), Seán Ó Tuama (1926–2006,), Art Ó Maolfabhail (1933), Seán Ó hÉigeartaigh (1931–2005), Pearse Hutchinson (1927–2013), Micheál Mac Liammóir (1899–1978), Réamon Ó Muireadhaigh (1938) and Caitlín Maude (1941–1982) challenged literary conventions and forged new strategies to deal with the global forces shaping Irish society.

Rosenstock and his coterie of kindred spirits—the *Innti* set—were emerging as Irish life was beginning to undergo turbulent transformations. The economic ease of the Lemass era and its new prosperity ushered in private yearnings for wider horizons and newer freedoms. Diverse and assertive voices were beginning to question the prevailing assumptions. There was a loss of confidence in inherited values whether social, political or religious. A gritty, urban youth culture was coming to the fore. It was a country slowly emerging from the oppressive domination of the Catholic Church. Still, that rigid and harsh institution held its moral sway over a whole range of human affairs. Emotions, ideas and creative expressions were still being stifled by a severe religious hierarchy. But change was in the air. Old cautious orders and stern, inflexible understandings were breaking up and giving way to a brash, youthful impulsiveness.

That change was reflected in Rosenstock's early work; a poetry of delightful impudence and waywardness, a sensibility that resided in the attitudes of youth and did not abide by what was traditionally and routinely acceptable. 'Freaked-out Pharoah' shows exactly how funky, defiant and free his work was at that time. He was taking Irish on a psychedelic trip:

Don't know
was it worth it.
Constipated, alleluia.

The gods are weeping in the temple of hashish, says D.
(Constipated also?)

Look around, you little poet you,
or
(failing that)
acquire some Arabic tongue or other
and ride the camel's back over balding ruins of sand.
Kiss the Sphinx!
Repeat three times
before retiring for the night . . .

I'm a Pharoah,
thy will be done on earth, O Lord—
sifting my body's dust.

—Translated by Gabriel Rosenstock

Susanne sa Seomra Folctha, his first collection of
poems, was published in the autumn of 1973. It is a
landmark book; a brazen, wildly inventive, eroti-
cally-charged volume; bursting with an irrepressible
urge to defy, to challenge settled habits of decorum
in style and in subject matter. The luscious nude sit-
ting in a steamy pose on the irreverently green
white and gold cover was indeed a bold statement
of intent. It was in stark contrast to the more som-
bre and modest images that beckoned from the cov-
ers of Irish-language books of the period. With a

certain licentious mirth this cover was saying that the time had come for Caitlín Ní Uallacháin to find her G-spot and exult in a lush Gaelic libido.

It is a book that announced the coming of a marvellously assured poet and signalled new beginnings in irish-language poetry. I would like to take a brief look at two pivotal poems from this volume. 'Deireadh Seachtaine na Martinis Dry' is a somewhat wry, urbane poem of social and sexual allure, very different in style, mood and tone to what was expected of an Irish language poem. Its setting, a soirée of world-weary, glib, modern day socialites was new to the ethos and experience of Irish. It is as much a commentary on the burgeoning of the *nouveau riche* in the Ireland of the late sixties as it is an account of an erotically charged encounter. It is very different, say, from the highly formalized free verse of Ó Direáin or the stunning, songlike intensity of a Máire Mhac an tSaoi poem. Rosenstock's poem expresses itself in an easy, off-handed manner but for all its ease and directness of speech it has a wiry vigour in its phrasing. Here, Gabriel is attuning the poem to the new rhythms of urban Irish and catching the excitements and appeal of that lingo. It is reminiscent of the freewheeling, fragmented style of Frank O'Hara's *Lunch Poems*—those midday, observational, stroll poems, through the intoxicating, thrills of Manhattan—and like them it glows with the same fresh, frank, spontaneous attentiveness to details. It's a poem that has kept its appeal and its iconic status for a whole generation of Irish poets who were coming of age at the

time of its appearance. It brilliantly catches some-
thing of the stir of those times and above all it still
holds the sensations of youth.The volume as a
whole was at variance with the folkloric and bucolic
character of much that was being written in Irish.
Here was a new youthful idiom; a trendy, roguish,
urban lingo underpinned by the *dúchas* but not, by
any means, entrapped by it. Rosenstock was coining
an Irish that was colourful and current, a speech
that was alive and had a slangy, *joie de vivre* street
cred about it. He wanted to have a less mannered,
more informal mode of poem than hitherto expe-
rienced in Irish; a kind of anti-poem that would
debunk the shibboleths of academia and the jingo-
istic myths of culture. He had the nerve and the
humour to air such laid-back baloney as "*Coinín,
Préachán, Colún, Asal/ Rabbit, Crow, Column, Donkey,*"
just to rattle the old fogies who had preconceived
notions of what a poem should be or not be.

> Did you ever see my sweetheart in her pyjamas?
> Yes indeed, she's always in pyjamas.
> just like a rabbit in the back garden.
> For months now I'm on the lookout for its tail.
>
> Did you ever see my beloved in her thighboots?
> Yes, thighboots I tell you.
> Jet black as a crow on a green lawn,
> Where is its nest? Upstairs of course.
>
> Did you ever see my adored one after a shower?
> Yes, a hot steamy shower.
> Just like a glorious white column you'd see in Rome.
> A column has no need of a towel.

Envoy:
If you see her tell her that . . .
Mention to that lass . . .
Tell her anything that comes into your head,
Say to her that she's a donkey, a useless bloody ass . . .

—*Translated by Cathal Ó Searcaigh*

Such lovely, saucy Rosenstockian insouciance! He would perfect that tone in later volumes and with it make an indelible mark on modern Irish poetry. The book opens, however, with a long poem, 'Laoi an Mheir-Indiaigh Dhíbeartha/ The lay of the displaced tribesman', one of the most moving works of modern Irish literature. It is a deeply imagined narrative; heartbreaking in its painful depiction of a heroic race reduced to impotence and ruin. This is the wretched of the earth, downtrodden and degraded by colonial greed and treachery; betrayed by land-grabbing governments; their culture shamefully wiped out, their self-esteem sapped, their lives reduced to drink, lethargy and dependency.

They doled out clay to bury our people;
The wind blows; I swallow the marrow of a race;

A drink for Gods sake!
Strength to wring drops from cactus.

They gave us new clothes to cover our shame;
The people's temple is razed; the totem seized by Frost.

We speak a different language, that chokes us
More than the endless dust spewing from the ravaged land.

It is a stark, unsettling poem that summons up the sheer agony and loss of a people who have their language, their customs, their way of life taken from them ruthlessly. It carries a rare quality of moral weight as it tries to make sense of the plight of these people, trapped in their own helplessness by the brutal forces and the unjust fate that impinges upon them with calamitous results. It is a sustained heartfelt lament, raw and blunt in its immediacy; a powerful outcry against the demeaning of human dignity.

When Gabriel was composing this poem in 1972/1973 there was a significant reappraisal of the Native American being effected in the media. The ruthless, scalp-hunting savage of so many Hollywood movies was slowly giving away to a more humane perception of these people. The pioneering film *Soldier Blue* and Dee Brown's engrossing bestseller *Bury my Heart at Wounded Knee* did much to dispel the ignominious myth of the bloodthirsty savage and to alert an ignorant public to the real story of these Native Peoples; to their culturally rich and varied tribal heritage and to their shameful extermination at the behest of a rapacious policy of State encroachment.

This outspoken poem of sympathy and indignation by Gabriel Rosenstock, and translated masterfully by Paddy Bushe, is an important addition to the writings that set the record straight on this shocking case of American ethnic cleansing.

It's a significant poem in Gabriel's ouvre, setting the scene for his abiding and ongoing engagement with the upheavals of history and the shadows cast by history.

***

There is something of the imaginative nimbleness and the deft narrative tact of the East European poets of the Iron Curtain era — a Rózewicz perhaps, or a Holub even — in the quirky and provocative stance he takes in 'Osclaím mo Dhán / I open my poem'.

It's from *Tuirlingt* (Descent), a book in which I shared equal billing with Gabriel. *Tuirlingt* was published in 1978. I'm not sure what I was descending from — perhaps the last bus to Gleann na nGealt. Anyway, my poems looked and sounded as if they had jumped off a vehicle in full flight. They were in shreds, concussed and incoherent. But unlike the indulgent, cryptic nonsense of my poems, Gabriel's work in that volume has a radiant ingenuity about it. A wonderful collision of ideas occur in his poems that make you view things anew. 'I open my poem' has an attractive naïveté and a considerable breath of vision. Behind its extempore childlike expression and its playful clowning I have no doubt but that it's a serious attempt to comment on the tumults of the times and to find an alternative delivery to deal with violent histories.

> . . . I open my poem to all the elements
> alive and dead and
> some ivy comes in trailing
> its own wall
> the wall falls on the cat
> this poem is a tragedy
> of sorts
> Somewhere in the world
> A wall is falling on a cat
> on a child
>
> I open my poem again to bright things
> but there's nothing left.

One of Gabriel's most admired poems is the superbly realized 'To my husband who is labouring on the Great Wall' from *Oráistí*, a volume of selected poems. He is always in search of emotional correlatives—plausible parallels from the remote past—that would allow him to make sense of the malaise of the present. It is a strategy that enables him to put his own life, and ours too, in a larger historical setting. In this poem we get a potted history, albeit an invented one, of a woman pining for her husband who is labouring on the Great Wall in a China that is struggling to safeguard its frontiers from attacking hordes. The poem is in the form of a love letter sent to the front; the cry of a woman separated from her beloved and fearful for his survival in the face of hardship and death. It is a tender, mournful message, speaking to us, as it were, across the abyss of the ages, about love and loneliness, grief and fear, the cruelty of war and its futility.

> . . . If only the moon would shine tonight
> and you—my heart's gleam—were watching it.
> Do they really think it will last forever?
> Against wind, against rain,
> Against frost, against the Barbarians?
> This countryside is under the sway of terror,
> just the other day
> A two-headed foal was born!

It is a glimpse of a barbarous era, not unlike our own, of unstoppable wars, strife and wretchedness, in which women and children are the forgotten victims. The poem is full of omens, superstitions, horrors, as happens when the natural order of things is convulsed and thrown into disarray. And it captures the dread and disquiet of a war-torn country. Truth, as we know, only too well, is the first casualty of war. Dissenting voices are silenced.

> Recent times have seen more men from this area
> Pressed into service. I will mention no names.
> Scholars and poets. Their scrolls were burned.
> They were roped together
> and, stonefaced, wordless, they set off for the north.

The abusive war propaganda that demonizes the enemy is always being spread:

> Is it true what they say about the Hseung-noo?
> That they eat their own young
> In times of shortage.
> That their palms sprout red fur?

The poem voices itself in a finely tuned, assured usage of Irish; beautifully graceful and yet, bold and daring in its delivery. We have a long tradition in the Irish language of swashbuckling, sabre-rattling poems full of reckless, heroic rhetoric. Gabriel eschews that kind of foolhardy bombast in favour of a more muted, subtle speech. And as a result he achieves a more humanely affecting poem.

Too often the work of major writers in the minority tongues is overlooked and is hardly ever included in the crucial and influential canonical anthologies. As an authoritative and telling war narrative this poem stands as a strong and convincing contender for all such inclusions.

***

Part of Gabriel's charm as a poet is his sensitivity to ethnic cultures elsewhere. Crossing boundaries and forging alliances with others is one of his foremost concerns. A widening out beyond the confines of Irish and a willingness to identify with other indigenous cultures has enriched the scope of his vision. He is Xolotl, an Aztec divinity with a Celtic outlook; he is with the pygmies, paying homage to the elephant; he is the hunchback dwarf in Montezuma's Inca court; he is a disaffected yeti and a visionary Sasquatch.

> Nothing but his own desires
> taught him how to read
> the stars
> he followed them
> they him

'STARS' from SASQUATCH

He is a poet who occupies many spaces and is, strange as it may seem, grounded in this diversity. He succeeds, somehow, in integrating a heady mix of the local and the global into a coherent and a cohesive vision. He is not so much an internationalist as a universalist. His allegiance is not so much to a particular race but to all of humanity. He is on the side of minority languages, marginalized tribes, outcasts, endangered species, threatened ecosystems.

His true homeland, it seems to me, is language rather than any geographical locale, and the fact that he is bound to language rather than to a flag or a particular piece of earth allows him to be boundless in his pursuits. Irish is not his mother tongue but he has immersed himself so much in the wellspring of Irish that he speaks with the expressiveness of a native speaker. He inhabits the language with grace, resides in it as securely as a tree in its bark and as snug as an animal in its skin.

As a poet he is very conscious of the tonal qualities of the language, the mantric properties inherent in it. He has learned much from the Irish tradition; the clear-sighted clarity of early Irish nature poems; the exquisitely fabricated interplay of sound and rhythm, assonance and alliteration of bardic poems; the thrilling sonority of 18th century love poems. He has used this knowledge to great effect in his poems, creating a compelling dialogue between the riches of the past and the fast-changing soundscapes of modern Irish. An experimenter in new forms and a new expressiveness, he nevertheless, upholds the vigorous continuity of the Irish poetic tradition. He is as capable of stanzaic elegance and a light formal control as he is of a wild, spacious *vers libre* spontaneity. 'Scairteann sé ar a aonsearc', from *Ní Mian léi an Fhilíocht Níos Mó* conveys an impeccable discipline and a bardic refinement reminiscent of the "laoithe cumainn".

SCAIRTEANN SÉ AR A AONSEARC

Fuar an chré orm, an leac is cruaidh
Tar is siúil ar m'uaigh go sámh,
Do dhá bhonn bhána mar bhalsam bisigh dom,
Crom orm arís, a Dheirdre án!

Can! Smiot oighearthost an gheimhridh,
Rinc! Is péacfaidh lá,
Léirscrios fógair ar ár naimhde,
Ríomh ár ngníomhartha gaisce i ndán.

Díbir deamhain dhorcha mo dhrólainne,
An t-uaigneas. An t-éad.An tnúthán.
Glaoigh as m'ainm orm "Naoise!"
Aon uair amháin.

Although he shuns any small-minded nationalist agenda, he is a ready campaigner for the rights of the language. Even though things have improved slightly, the reality is that Irish is still on the margins of the mainstream literary scene in Ireland. And Gabriel has been a keen and tireless voice in our struggle for literary visibility. His well-known poem 'A Portrait of the Artist as a Yeti' tackles this predicament with irresistible wit and a sweet, sad wistfulness. The poem showcases all of Gabriel's poetic strengths — his inventiveness, his ability to make unexpected connections, his sense of the absurd and his persuasive rhythmic charm. All of that is brought to bear on the quandary of being an artist, an outsider, "neither man nor beast". In his uniquely peculiar style Gabriel succeeds in saying something pertinent about the Irish language writer lost between two languages, two cultures, two worlds.

***

Ní Mian léi an Fhilíocht Níos Mó, a book of frenzied, enraptured love poems from 1993, the most sustained expression of sexual desire in modern Irish literature. By turns gothic, demonic, shamanic, these poems address the beloved with an obsessive fervour. From first sight to last *"slán"*, through moods of anxiety, moments of euphoria, beguiling joys and forbidden desires, the poet's rapt gaze follows this capricious play, this carnalia, with savage intensity. You get the impression from the poems that it's an experience of desire well beyond the social strictures; an abandoned and exultant merging with the Muse.

> You have chosen death in life
> before life in death with me
>
> — *'The shadowy crypts of your soul'*

It is a book of voluptuous lyricism, delicate and fiery sometimes, rancorous and spiteful at other times but always shot through by a lush, alluring melody.

> As I drain into you
> It will generate such heat
> That I will crystallize in you:
> Crystal upon crystal
> Taking shape in you
> Coming and going in you
> Here and there, there and here,
> Like sunshine between showers, until
> My very essence is distilled.

— *'Science lesson'*

He knows that the redemptive rapture of the erotic union is when we are most in touch with the life force, and, despite what institutionalised religions say and teach, the poet knows, that the flesh can enlighten and edify the spirit.

From *Syójó* (2001) onwards his poetry is a realm of mythic beings. Xolotl, Krishnamurphy, the Goddess, Sasquatch, inhabit his consciousness. He has always been in touch with the ancient wisdom of antiquity, whether Indian, Celtic, Chinese, Mayan but now, through a heterogeneous array of guises he embodies that knowledge; he gives it a new utterance. Some ineffable essence permeates these poems; a vibratory force and a resonance that is hypnotic and oracular. There is also in these poems a belief that the rhythmic pulsations of words—the mantric source of poetry

—is restorative and healing. A belief that poems can rouse us up and embolden the sluggish heart and the slack mind to open up to the Sublime; to get out of our confined selfhood and taste immense existence.

> Every poem written for you
> Is the one poem
> One breath
> One word, one syllable
> One star
> Among all heavenly bodies
> In a limitless sky
> One fragrance
> Among all
> Since it is You
> That gives Fragrance to the word
> That surpasses meaning
> Beyond the stars
> Beyond the word
> That shines in me
>
> —*from 'One poem'*

Gabriel is truly open to the Word, welcoming its mysteries, realizing it can connect us to the sacred and the cosmic, to the local and the astral. Poetry prevails where institutional religion fails. In recent volumes, *Syójó* (2001), *Year of the Goddess* (2007), *Sasquatch* (2013), his poetry speaks with the mystical fervour of a Kabir or a Rumi. They are the poems of the inner voyager, of an individual yearning for true liberation, for unnameable Bliss.

Here we have poems that deliberately evade the intellect and connect with a deeper instinctive strain within the psyche. They are poems that go beyond the limiting conventions of our creeds and speak to us with the glorious unorthodoxy of the mystic Fool.

Bliain an Bhandé/ Year of the Goddess (2008) is both a tantric and a gnostic hymn to the Sacred Feminine —that liberating, instinctual life-force that is so abhorrent to the patriarchal power bases of our society. It is a poem full of the wonder and adoration of a person who intuits the divine dance of energy that permeates Creation. It is a pertinent poem for our times when the healing wisdom of the Feminine is surely needed to cure humanity; to free it from self-hating codes of belief and creeds with repressive ethics and to guide it into a bounteous consciousness of Love; a culture of compassion and care.

Gabriel's poetry teems with an abundance of fauna and flora especially in his haiku and his children's verse. (He is our very own Edward Lear of Irish literature.) He has always been strong on global ecological issues and in his work he laments our loss of natural diversity. The earth that nurtures us also needs nurturing. Now, more than ever, it needs holistic healthcare. *Sasquatch* (2013) is a sequence of poems by a mystic anthropoid who gives uncanny insights into the plight of his ever-vanishing habitats. In short, aphoristic poems he gives stern testimony to what happens when we denude our world of its wonderful biodiversity.

***

Since the beginning of his career Gabriel has an affinity with the Japanese arts and its aesthetics. He has devoted much of his energies to the writing and the promotion of Haiku and is now Ireland's pre-eminent haijin and its most authoritative and inspiring teacher.

The classical Japanese haiku is a mere seventeen syllables of brevity and formal delicacy. It speaks with the dazzle of a raindrop dripping from a bough. For the haikuist it's a question of seeing; being attentive to the immediate. He becomes by virtue of seeing, a visionary of the real.

Strange as it may seem, the haiku is not at all alien to the Irish literary tradition. Its anti-discursive stance and its delight in the natural world is akin to early Irish monastic lyrics; those poems of formal concision and clarity from the sixth, seventh and eight centuries; written by monks and hermits, ascetics who achieved a high degree of attentiveness in their lives. These luminous moments of theirs tell us how to evoke things by suggestion, how to be emotive without being sentimental and slushy. Just like the haiku, the same attentive mindset.

I can see its attraction for Gabriel. The haiku—a lesson in compactness and insight—is indeed an endorsement of his own world view: in order to savour the full potential and promise of being you have to remain open and attentive.

Gabriel's vast oeuvre of haiku contains many memorable compositional delights. Here is one:

> bláthanna i vása
> siúlann cat
> trí gharraí lom

> flowers in a vase
> a cat walks
> in a bare garden

I love the clear, uncluttered brevity of that. It's purity of attention. It rings with the clarity of a little Buddhist temple bell. A poem like this makes us aware, and by doing just that it broadens our compassion, deepens our care and extends our sympathy out to all that lives and coexists with us on this earthly habitat.

> maidin sheaca
> nochtann spideog a brollach
> don saol Fódlach

> frosty morning
> a robin bares her breast
> to the wide world

There it is: an experience made vivid. Like Japanese painting, it has a minimalist approach to subject matter, a landscape by Hokusai for instance; a few lines of ink and a whole scene is evoked, alive and vibrant. It is interesting how Paddy Bushe — a distinguished, prize-winning haikuist — translates the last line. 'Fódlach' pertains to Ireland and is a common idiomatic expression in Irish, meaning 'the whole country'. But Paddy, to avoid any awkwardness, opts for a comparable phrase in English, something that is equally simple and idiomatic. 'To the wide world' is an agreeable match for the Irish idiom. A good translator amplifies the text rather than altering it.

***

The bringing of a poem from one language across the abyss to another language is a hazardous journey but in the capable hands of Paddy Bushe a poem can be assured of a safe passage, a successful crossing. There are many kinds of translations—versions, re-tellings, imitations—but Mr Bushe will have none of these. He strives for fidelity, for attaining close equivalence. Like Dryden, he favours keeping the sense of the words; this sense can be amplified but not altered. Even in poems that exist wholly in the purity of their diction and in the subtlety of their rhythmic modulations—the most difficult of all poems to translate—he manages to imbue them with the same charge and tension that is achieved in the original. In a short poem like 'Gála'/ 'Gale', a lovely exercise in euphony, Paddy shows us what an inventive mediator he is between the two languages:

> Cleatráil doirse is fuinneog
> deatach, dusta, duilleoga,
> tá an lá ina ghála
> aondomhan gan fál.

doors and windows are tumultuous,
leaves and smoke and swirling dust,
the day is blowing helter-skelter
and it's all one world without shelter.

He has reconstituted the poem in a diction that is commensurate with the original and in doing so has produced a valid poem in English that has the same cadences, the stress and pitch of the Irish. A bilingual reader will immediately grasp how apt the translation is but for the non-speaker of Irish it would take a tedious language lesson to elucidate the rightness of it. Suffice to say that Paddy by a linguistic sleight of hand flicks the original into credible English. The only way to translate a poem like this, as Auden said, is to write well.

Poetry is language articulating itself at its most acute. Each word glows with its own rainbow of meanings. It's difficult for a translator to capture all those tones and textures of colour. A whole range of sub-textual lore may be contained in a word but how is a translator to evoke even a hint of those riches? Paddy Bushe accomplishes this task wondrously.

Labhráimid teanga eile a thachtann sinn
Níos mó ná síoraiseag smúite an talaimh bhánaithe.
Fuaim na gcos ag damhsa, ró-annamh, róleochaileach,
Gliogar glan á chur le seanfhonn eolchaireach.
Tobac saor ag sreamacháin athmheilte go fulangach.

—*from 'Laoi an Mheir-Indiaigh Dhíbeartha'*

We speak a different language, that chokes us
More than the endless dust spewing from the ravaged land.
The thud of dancing feet too rare, too lifeless,
An old air of exile becoming pure jingle!
No-hopers passively chewing dole tobacco.

—*from 'The Lay of the Displaced Tribesman'*

By any standard that is an impressive translation. It achieves the twin feats of being literally faithful and poetically charged. It is so attuned to the original that it carries the same gestures of language and the same movement of words. Let us consider the phrase "*an talaimh bhánaithe*" meaning in Irish 'whitened', 'depopulated', 'cleared out', 'laid waste', 'emptied', or 'devastated' land. From this range of expressive possibilities Paddy opts for a word that embodies all of the above but is even more revealing. 'Ravaged land' is a weightier choice, a more forceful, compelling idea and its similar to the sentiment of the original. Likewise with the phrase "*seanfhonn eolchaireach*". 'Eolchaireach' itself is a literary word with an ancient feel to it, a rich and rare word, not in common usage. It means homesickness, grief, lamentation, longing, sadness, home love. '*Seanfhonn*' literally translated means 'old tune'. Again Paddy comes up with a cogent equivalent in English, "an old air of exile". It's a perceptive choice. You could spend a long time praising the merits of that one verse, how each word is assiduously chosen to correspond with the original; how the musical phrasing catches something of the timbre of Irish, how the translator himself takes delight in his labour.

Gabriel Rosenstock is our greatest Gaelic traveller across linguistic and cultural borders. His numerous translations into the Irish language attest to that. He once remarked that translation was like a blood transfusion between friends. In that vein the present enterprise between himself and Paddy Bushe is hugely invigorating.

"*Tuirsionn na Himáilithe mé*" changes from slangy Irish into "*the Himalayas wreck my head*", an equally slap-happy colloquialism. And in 'Syójó' look at how "*Bodach an Chóta Lachtna*" a fabulous character from the Fenian lore—but unknown to the ordinary English speaker—becomes the much more textually understood Mr Hyde. '*Seek and you will find*' is Mr Bushe's motto.

And in these marvelous translations he brilliantly catches the stir and sparkle of Rosenstock as that sage freewheels his way around the world, divinely intoxicated by the light of other cultures.

Gabriel Rosenstock is an extraordinary presence where East and West meet in a full frontal benediction of the Word. Wherever he is, a sense of wonder informs his vision. He is blessed and he believes in living the faith of poetry. He's on a high in the flea market in Valparaiso, his mule drinks from the Ganges, and Semiramis casts him a glance. For the past forty years he has been taking the Irish language on amazing journeys into unfamiliar realms; unchartered spaces of the imagination beyond which no *Modh Coinníollach* ever ventured. And he continues to roam the dark depths of words and the bright harbours of sound. He chants from the Way of the White Cloud, hymns of light. Out of a limitless universe of language he shines on all of us—a Gaelic sunburst.

Dhoirtis grá
Is bhí an uile ní faoi bhláth

You poured love
and everything blossomed.

3. Upbringing

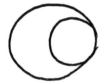

The Well

We had a well below the house.

It was hidden in a ferny nook underneath a drystone wall. You had to kneel down on a flat stone, dip the bucket into it and haul up the water. When I carried it in a white enamel pail, it became a breathy shininess that sloshed about and brimmed over like a shoal of silver fish.

On sunny days, the light gave it a coat of dazzle, making it into a shiny mirror. On those days, thirsty for a drink, I'd lie on my belly and slurp up my own face out of its cool sweetness. It was a moist cave with the same sweet—sour odour I got off my mother when I laid my head in her lap; a damp fragrance that was oddly comforting. Mossy green at the sides and rust-red where, at the back, a gurgle of water spilled out of a rock, it was a restful place to put your head into.

On no account would my mother allow water to be carried into the house after dark. It was unlucky. At night it was better to stay away from the well, she advised me. During the daytime it was ours, but at night it belonged to the *slua sí*, the fairies. Anything could happen to you there, she stressed, at that uncanny hour.

"Look at what happened to Domhnall na Gealaí," she warned me. Domhnall was a youngster who always went to the well at night to fetch a bucket of water, against his mother's better judgement it must be said. One night, the moon whooshed down, seized him and carried him off to the sky. On clear nights, I could make him out, standing at a crossroads, a sack on his back, staring blankly ahead. I felt sorry for him, all alone on that lonely moon. Sometimes I'd point a torch at him and flash a friendly wave just to show him that somebody was thinking about him. I wondered could my wee light really slash at the dark and make a bright path up through the night to where he stood, dithering over which road to take. But now and again a flicker in his glassy eye was enough to convince me that contact was being made. As well as that, having a nodding acquaintance with Domhnall na Gealaí made that far-off moon seem less distant.

From time to time my father and I cleaned out the well. With tin buckets, we drained it dry and then scooped up the ooze and slobber that clotted the bottom of it. *"Clear water comes from a clean well,"* he'd tell me. *"Aye, boy, you've to care for the source."* He always threw in a sprinkling of lime to purify it. *"Always think of the well when you're drinking the water,"* he would counsel me.

Once, when we were bucketing out the well, he tossed the water in a wide arc behind him and created one glittering rainbow after another.

"How do you make a rainbow, Daddy?" I asked him, astounded at what was happening in front of me.

"I don't rightly know," he said modestly. He peered around as if groping for an answer. Across the glen, a pale sun shivered behind damp clouds. *"I just fling the water at the sun,"* he said and laughed at the simplicity of it. I wanted to be a rainbow-maker too, just like my daddy. I took my bucket in my hands and flung the water up into the air the way he was doing it but no matter how much I tried, it wouldn't rainbow for me. Again with an easy swerve, he slung the water out and up and instantly it curved into a glowing bow of colours. Frustrated, I broke out sobbing.

"Why can't I do it, Daddy?" I complained bitterly.

"Och, I don't know, a thaisce," and he gave me a mournful look.

"*It's just pot luck,*" he said, trying to console me. "*You throw it in the air and if you're lucky, it catches the light. It's all in the slant, I think, and the timing.*"

He suggested we try it together. We gripped the bucket, my father on one side, me on the other. "*Righto,*" he urged and we tossed the glistening water into the air, and for one magical moment it flared up into a flashy rainbow and then was gone. Brief but perfect. We looked at each other in Wonder.

"*We made a rainbow, Daddy!*"

"*Aye, boy, a well-made rainbow, you could say,*" and he guffawed delightedly at his own Wordplay. Brimming with joy, I also broke out laughing. Something strange had happened, I felt, at that moment, something delicately rare and pure as if we had overflowed into one another.

We tried it again but never managed to make a second rainbow. Soon, the evening light waned and gave way to dusk and then, like net curtains being drawn, a fine drizzle closed around us.

THE WELL
for Máire Mhac an tSaoi

'That'll put the jizz back in you,'
said old Bríd, her eyes glinting,
as she handed me a bowl of real water
from the purest well in Gleann an Átha.
A well kept sweet and neat
by her people's people, the precious
legacy of the household, tucked away in a nook,
a ditch around it for protection,
a flagstone on its mouth.

Here, in the early sixties
just as I came into my strength
there wasn't a house in the district
without a well like this. Everyone
so proud of how sweet and cool
they kept the family well. They'd allow
no glut or *glár* to gather in it
and a trace of rust was reason
enough to bail it out at once with tin
buckets. Each quarter day without
fail, they'd kiln-lime it sweet.

The lucid gush of a true spring
burst and plashed from my people's well.
When we were consumed by thirst
and struck with summer's sweat
we took it daily by bowl and pitcher.
It slacked and cooled us in fields
and bog. It throbbed through us
like a tonic—gave us life and laughter.
It washed us all, from the infant's
first bath to the corpse's last cleaning.

But for a long time now there is a snake
of pipe that sneaks in from distant hills
and in every kitchen, both sides
of the glen, water spits from a tap;
bitter water without spark
that leaves a bad taste in the mouth
and among my people
the real well is being forgotten.

'It's hard to find a well these days,'
said old Bríd, filling up my bowl again.
'They're hiding in rushes and juking in grass,
all choked up and clatty with scum
but for all the neglect they get
their mettle is still true.
Look for your own well, pet,
for there's a hardtime coming.
There will have to be a going back to sources.'

—Translated by the author

The Derry Boat

My father is on the floor on all fours, and I'm astride him, riding high and happy. He trots hoppity-hop along the flagstones, doing the round of the kitchen. He neighs and then lets on to be champing the bit and rattling his harness. I hold on tightly to the reins of his galluses, click my tongue and tease him forward. "*Giddy up, Betty. Giddy up, horsey.*" He speeds up into a gentle gallop, then all of a sudden stalls and I come tumbling off his back in skraiks of laughter.

"*You call yourself a cowboy, do ye?*" he taunts me, then sits me on his knees and tickles me absently, half-heartedly, as if his attention is elsewhere. Usually, I'm pleading for mercy, his tickling is so lively and vigorous. When I look at him I notice that something is amiss in his face; it has lost its colour, its ruddy glow. It has become pale grey and pasty like the dough Mammy makes.

"I'm going away to Scotland tomorrow," he says cautiously.

Scotland, although I didn't know where it was exactly, was a place that was familiar to me. I had heard so much about it from my parents, who had worked there before they were married. I knew that it was a place where people went, men mostly, when they needed work. Nevertheless, it took me by surprise. The disclosure was so sudden, so strange and dangerous. I was dropped in the middle of no place and in the dark of night left to wander where there was no light and no human warmth.

"When will you be back?" I asked, rubbing the rough, spiky stubble on his jaw with a nervous finger.

"In five months or thereabouts," he said.

"How long is five months, Daddy?" He gave a soft sigh and his eyes moistened.

"Not too long, a chroí, when you're out playing every day."

My heart was in a flutter as if a little bird was trapped in my ribcage. I could hear the dip and rise of it and I thought it was going to burst out through my mouth any minute. That night, lying between them in bed, I held on to my father with a pressing neediness, not wanting to lose the warm sureness of his presence. I wished that the night would dawdle, linger here and there, mooch about in the moonlight and forget about the morning. I was annoyed at the tick-tock urgency of the clock ushering in the dawn. When the light began to seep through a chink in the curtains, a feeling of hopelessness came over me. Daylight would take him away from me.

There was a cold nip in the air when I went out to pee behind the house. The sun was like a shiny copper penny standing on its edge above Andy's Hill. I knew that my father was going to Scotland to earn some money so that we wouldn't be as hard up as we were. Nearly all the neighbouring men went; that was how things were for grown-ups, I guessed. Taking the Derry boat was part of their lives. I wished that we weren't so poor; then my father wouldn't have to go away. I prayed that, somehow, we would fall into money; that a legacy would, unexpectedly, come our Way. Didn't my Auntie Mary in Mín Doire na Slua say that we had rich relatives in faraway Montana? I asked God would He mind taking one of them up to heaven, but not before they had left us a big lab in their will. The fierce squawk of a crow as it swished out of the trees behind the henhouse frightened me, and I scampered back to the kitchen. Maybe it was a sign of disapproval from God for demanding such an awful thing, but then again it could have been a hint that He had given the go-ahead to my desperate request.

My mother was up and doing her best to be cheerful, but sometimes her words faltered and she'd turn away and wipe her eyes with the hem of her apron. She made porridge and sweetened mine with a more-than-usual sprinkling of sugar. I began to like the rasp and scratch of her spoon as she scraped the pot for *scriobogaí*, the burnt scourings that my father liked. Every other morning the grind of it grated on my nerves, but now it was a sound I associated with him and it was comforting. His early-morning clatter around the house usually woke me up and left me grumpy. Now I was going to miss all that morning din of his, the creek of byre doors opening and closing and the racket of tin buckets in the yard as he tended the cattle.

We sat around the fire eating Mammy's stodgy porridge and chatting about the journey that he was about to make. Talking settled my nerves and distracted me. He would take the Loch Swilly bus to Derry, he said, have a bite and a sup in Molloy's, close to the Diamond, and then sail on the *Lairds Loch**, a cattle ship to Glasgow. He would stay for a day or two with Auntie Biddy in Ballater Street and then head on up to Haddington by bus. He knew all the farms around there and would easily find work. I longed to see the little towns whose names tripped off my father's tongue like fabulous enchantments: East Linton, Stenton, Chirnside, Dunbar, Duns, Grantshouse. And the farms themselves—Beanston Mains, Harelaw, Morkel, Belgrange, The Knowes, Abbey Mains—were magical domains,

* MV Lairds Loch was sold to Israel in 1969 and was attacked by Arab frogmen shortly afterwards. She ran aground the following year in the Gulf of Aqaba and that was the end of her!

ablaze with the rich yield of their wheat fields. When he talked about handling horses I could hear the trot and clatter of Clydesdales across cobbled farmyards. He told me that a single potato field in Beanston Mains was as big as all the fields of Mín 'a Leá rolled into one.

After breakfast, my mother stood on a chair and took down the dingy, brown cardboard suitcase that was stored atop the high press in the bedroom, dusted it off and began to pack it with *"Daddy's ould duds,"* as she said: his brown corduroy trousers, a bulky gansey, some shirts and an old tweed jacket, his báinín, waistcoat and a pair of scruffy, hobnailed boots which she scrubbed clean before putting them in. At ten o'clock, clean-shaven and wearing his Sunday best—a light-blue, double-breasted suit, a crisp white shirt and a cap—he was ready to leave.

When we faced each other to say farewell, I thought the floor was quaking under me. Everything was in a hopeless wobble. He clasped my hand and said, *"You're the man of the house now. Be good to Mammy and look after her, won't you?"*

"Cheerio, Daddy. I'll be thinking of you every day," I gulped out, at a loss for words.

"I'll write as soon as I get settled on a farm, Agnes," he said, hugging my mother who was now weeping loudly.

He lifted the battered suitcase and walked out, head down and expressionless, without looking at us. We stood in the doorway watching him go. At the cow byre, he turned around and waved. The sun shone on his scrubbed face and we could make out big smudges on his cheeks. He was crying. Then he hopped over a ditch and was gone.

An old pair of his tweed trousers hung limp on a hook behind the kitchen door. I buried my head in them and cried my eyes out. Afterwards, I felt that a little bit of me fell away and disappeared in the tears the way a small peaty *bruach* collapsed sometimes and fell into the *Dúloch*, the Black Lake. That was what people meant by loss. You lost something of yourself and you had to replace it with something else; otherwise you drained away and shrivelled up.

The Cow Byre

It was a clammy morning at the tail end of July. A low, grey cloud with a stippling of brown and pink hung over the hills like a distended udder. My mother was in the cow byre milking. I could hear the hum and purr of her voice as she sang a *suantraí*, an irish lullaby, to settle the cows. When I was a baby she always sang that song to hush and soothe me when I cried. Now it lulled me again into a deep sense of contentment as I entered the byre and sat down beside her on a small three-legged stool. I didn't mind the cobwebbed murk of the place or the whiff of dank straw and the stench of skittery dung that filled my nostrils. It was exciting to sit close to my mother in that breathy half-light and watch her tug and squeeze those teats of mottled pink and see spurts of warm milk thwacking into the tin bucket that was wedged between her bare, bony knees. The sweaty mystery of it roused me. The jerk of teat and spew of milk done with a steady drag of the hand, the heave and slump of the cows breathing, the rise and fall of my mother's song made my heart thump in a way that I had never experienced before. I felt a hot urgency in my chest as if a bud of fire had opened up within me, a sweet, burning pressure that made me blush. Why, I didn't know. Suddenly a beat, a rhythm, a word stirred in me, a palpitating thrust as pressing as the push of a root through stodgy soil. And then the tingle and pulse of words as they gushed out of me.

Cowmothermorning. Milksongbyre. Dunglightpoem.

I was giving voice to something inasmuch as the gibberish I uttered meant anything. Cadence became deliverance and I felt a jolt of wild joy shooting up my body as I chanted the words out loud so that my mother, the two cows and the stones of the byre could hear them.

Cowmothermorning. Milksongbyre. Dunglightpoem.

The gasp and grunt of them coming out of my mouth made me tremble. I was scattering seeds in a new field, tiny grains of sound, seedlings of sense. The cows gazed at me with big, still eyes streaked with silver. My mother turned around, ripples of soft light like a hand smoothing down her thick, wavy hair. She dipped her finger in the bucket and blessed herself with the bright creamy froth. She always did that when she had finished the milking.

"*Are you praying?*" she said, giving me a wry smile. It hadn't occurred to me that what I was saying was a prayer. I thought of it more as a poem, but now it crossed my mind that maybe a poem and a prayer were one and the same. They were both ways of talking to God. At church they were very strict about the saying of prayers. Prayers were to be revered. They were set words, solid as holy rocks in the huge mind of God and they could not be changed. We had to say them as they were, faithfully and accurately.

"*Was that a prayer, Mammy?*" I asked her, startled at the idea that my own words could be one. I thought that only saints could make up prayers, pure devouts who glimpsed the sacred texts hanging in the chapels of heaven.

"*I don't know, a chroí, but you were reelin' it off like a litany at a wake,*" she said, untethering the cows and letting them out to graze around the byre. Through the open doorway a faint yellowy light glided into the byre, hovered over us and then was gone. For a moment the place glowed as if an angel had looked in on us.

IN THE COWBYRE

The cowbyre is alive
with the milk of her words.

Her udder is heavy
as a dictionary;
her breath as measured
as a Dán Díreach.

Out in the field
she drinks her fill
of the sky's blue vowels
and grazes on green syllables of grass.

With her tail she conducts
a *chorus angelorum* of flies
and with her holy low
gives praise
to her thrush's morning hymn.

I savour the pure cream
of her poetry
in my mother's milk bucket.

—Translated by the author

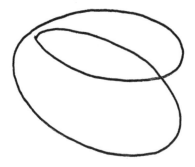

The Artist

Madge is an artist and she lives away out in Prochlais. The grey bulk of Eachla Mhór rears its horsey head to the sky across the valley from her house. Her gleaming white cottage on a craggy rise is sited between a fairy wood and a dark bog lake. It's a summer's day and my mother and I are visiting her. We took the short cut across the ridge, a mile or so of a tramp through dry, stumpy heather, to bring her a clutch of duck eggs for hatching.

The frail tendrils of woodbine that cling to the stone wall of her yard are as delicate as the fingers of a wee girl trying to climb up the wall and see what is on the other side. She is also like that, I think, full of a lively curiosity about things. She stands in the doorway, a stout woman in a green floral dress, and enthuses about the lilies that are blooming in her small plot of flowers.

"Look at them lilies! Aren't they pretty?"

My mother and I gaze at them with delight. They are velvety white tongues humming with bees.

"Come on in for a wee drop of tea," she says in a soft, unhurried voice, motioning us into her kitchen. A big red geranium on the table fills the place with a sharp, tangy scent. I notice a picture of a boldly drawn Errigal hanging on the wall by the window, coloured in what looks like cigarette foil silver. The sky above it is a pink glisten of clouds and the bottom veers off into a purple fleck of bog.

"Do you recognise that mountain?" she asks me. It's more a tactic to get me talking, I realise, than a question.

"That's Errigal," I say.

"I did that one last week. It's a damn hard mountain to catch."

"Why?" I ventured, forgetting my shyness.

"Because it keeps changing its face. With every shift of light it gets a new one. Errigal has more faces on it than a crowd at a Celtic football match." She peers at me with an inquisitive eye and asks, *"What do you see in this Errigal?"*

I look down at the floor, unsure of what to say. *"It's like a . . . silver jug with a . . . a piece of pink soap on top of it,"* I stammer out at last.

She laughs at that and says to my mother, *"Agnes, that boy has an eye."*

"Aye, like meself, he sees what's not there more than he sees what's there," my mother says as she removes the duck eggs from her shopping bag and places them carefully in a deep, yellow bowl on the dresser.

"I hope these hatching eggs will be lucky for you, Madge. You've got great scope here for ducks with the water and all beside you!"

"It's grand, Agnes, except that the fox is always on the prowl. Yesterday, he nabbed another of my hens."

I sit by the settle bed and stroke a small tawny cat that purrs contentedly on a tasselled cushion at my feet while the two women natter away. Madge wets the tea in a bulbously fancy teapot, lets it draw and then pours it gracefully into dainty blue cups.

"I bought this willow-pattern tea set at a sale in Glasgow," she tells my mother. She hands me a cup. It's scalding hot. I wince with pain and the cup slips through my sliddery fingers and cracks into little shimmering flickers of delph on the flagstoned floor. My heart is pumping hard with fright. This is my first time in her house and I've smashed her precious tea cup.

"You're a wee clouster, so you are," my mother says, reprimanding me. I want to get away from what I've done. I rush out the door and scramble up the hill behind the house, sobbing.

"Come down here, you wee scrunt and don't be actin' the maggot," my mother shouts up at me. Dolly, Madge's old shaggy donkey, is munching wisps of grass beside me. Her face looks sad and mournful like the cheerless face of Jesus in the Stations of the Cross. I look away and hear the drone of bees in the heather. It's like the dull hum of penitents in the church when they murmur their prayers after confession. It rankles in my ear. I get a tightening in the pit of my stomach when I see my mother and Madge clambering up the slope to where I'm sitting.

"I'm sorry, Madge, I'm sorry," I cry out in gulping sobs.

"It's alright, you've only broken a silly wee cup, dear." Her voice is kind and tender. She pats my flushed cheeks and smooths back my tangle of sweaty curls. Mother takes my hand and coaxes me down the brae. Back in the kitchen, Madge takes out a flat tin box full of a glossy, wet mess of colours and a thick leaf of sheeny paper.

"I'm going to paint a wee picture of Prochlais for you," she says, grinning at me with a ready enthusiasm. I sit at the table beside her and watch her work. She holds a slender brush in her hand, daubs it in her box of wet paints and stains the paper with a dribble of colour. A splodge of brown, a dash of blue, a

smear of grey, a glob of green and there is Prochlais gleaming at me in a wash of colours. It's all there, the lake, the bog, the scatter of houses, the stony hulk of a mountain. It's the first time I witness an artist at work. It fills me with wonderment to see her sitting at the table rapt in her painting like a saint praying or like the visionary I saw in the church magazine, his face aglow with whatever he was seeing. Perhaps she too is a miracle worker. If she can put a landscape together so effortlessly, I think to myself, maybe she can put the shattered cup together again. I gaze around her cool, delph-bright kitchen and feel better about myself.

"*A wee view of Prochlais for yourself. I hope you like it,*" she said and handed me the finished picture. Her voice is a sweet curl of vine that trails itself around me and cheers me up. I take the picture in my hand and peer at it. Up close it looks like a gloopy muddle of colours but when I hold it out at arm's length I see Prochlais plain as day.

"*It's lovely, Madge,*" I beam up at her reassuringly. Then on a sudden impulse I hug her. She laughs out loud and places a big dollop of a kiss on my cheek. She has moist, shiny eyes that ooze with light like the dark, sweet syrup that my mother spreads on my bread sometimes.

"*It's the first time I got a hug for one of my pictures but I hope it's not the last one,*" she confides in me, then grins, and with her fingers, gently tweeks my cheek.

After we say our goodbyes she stands at the corner of her sunlit house and I keep waving to her until we round a bend in the road.

Below us, the fairy wood of Prochlais, a rambling tangle of ash, hazel and sally slopes down to the Sweeneys' farm. It is a screen of green that covers one side of the hill. As always it is eerily quiet. Even the birds, it seems to me, have kept away from it. Maybe they too are fearful of disturbing its green silence. The wood was '*uasal*', enchanted, and none of the locals would cut down a tree in it nor would they pick its nuts and berries or gather firewood there for fear of vexing the wee folk. My mother told me that they didn't live there, it was just a way in, an opening to their world.

It occurred to me as we were passing that the fairies were good to Madge and maybe even gave her a helping hand with her painting. I broached this with my mother.

"*They don't do her any bad, that's for sure,*" she answered with a wry smile. "*Madge keeps a good eye on their property and they keep an eye on her. Anyway, she has the eye for painting.*"

"*Maybe the fairies gave her a magical eye, Mammy, so that she can see more colour than anybody else.*" I was holding her Prochlais in my hand. It was interesting to see both of them at the same time, the painted Prochlais and the actual Prochlais. It was clear that

Madge saw a more delicate range of colours than what was visible to me. She saw tints of red and hints of yellow where I saw nothing but a murky bog brown. Until that day I thought of Prochlais as a place shadowed by mountains, stark and scant of light. Madge opened my eyes to a Prochlais that was a shock of startling colours.

"I know a woman who got a song off the síogaí," my mother said as we veered off the road and cut across the bog. *"And a fiddler who got the gift of a tune. I never heard word of them meddling with paints, but who knows what the new breed will be like."*

Coming down by Loch an Ghainimh we came across a dead sheep, a spongy mass of rotting flesh lying in the heather. There was a swirl of flies buzzing around the stink and when I looked closer I saw a white glisten of maggots moving in the mire. Normally such a sight would sicken me but that evening I made little of it. I was so enthralled by my picture that a smelly sheep wasn't going to bother me.

When I got home I found an old battered frame in the barn with a fading holy picture in it. I took the picture out, polished up the frame as best I could and fitted Prochlais into it. Unbeknownst to myself I was becoming a devotee of art rather than of religion. I placed the framed picture on the mantel-piece in our bedroom right between two brown china dogs.

As it happened that was my first and only contact with Madge. Soon after that she sold out, left Prochlais and went to live in faraway Ramelton. My father pointed it out on the map and said it would take the best part of a day to get there by bus. On the map it was just a dot, a speck of black on the wiggly blue of Lough Swilly. *"She's had enough of them lonely hills. Now she wants to make a life for herself down there by the sea,"* was how my mother explained her going away. I was sad when she left. Without her Prochlais would be a lonelier place.

However, I had her picture and when I looked at it I saw a Prochlais where earth and sky clasped each other in a hug of light. That lifted my spirits.

I would sit sometimes on the rise above our house and watch the lingering touch of sunlight on the curve of a cloud and imagine that Madge was watching the same thing in Ramelton.

At School

English was the only subject that really got me
going, and that was due to Mr Lally and the way he
conducted his class with dash and gusto. The oomph
with which he said things made the blood pound in
my head with excitement. Other classes may have
been drearily predictable, but his never failed to
surprise. I remember him, for instance, taking a
reel-to-reel tape recorder into our class and playing
us ocean sounds; the boom of water breaking on
rocks, the cry of gulls and a long slush of waves
across a pebbly strand. He got us to act out what we
heard. Spread out over the classroom, we became a
squawking, wing-flapping ocean in motion. He
would recite 'Dover Beach', he told us, a poem by
Matthew Arnold, but it would be a good idea, he
suggested, to let the poem come into the five ports

173

of our senses as if it were the sea. In this way we would become more conscious of the language of the poem, its tumultuous sound waves, its dark depths, its ceaseless dazzle. As he recited I let the poem flow into me. Suddenly I was afloat on a wave of language; in touch with the heave and surge of syllables, the murmurings of vowels, the rumblings of consonants.

In my second year at the tech the Department of Education authorised a new and broader curriculum in vocational schools, which allowed us to stay on for five years and study for the Leaving Cert. The new syllabus retained the practical subjects but introduced a wide range of academic options. Mr Lally, knowing how unhandy I was at woodwork, metalwork and Technical Drawing, got me out of doing these subjects.

It was a relief to be freed from my own fumbling incompetence at the workbench and the drawing board. Instead, I took History and Latin, Geography, Maths, Biology, Irish and English.

It was a fabulous five-year voyage of discovery, with Mr Lally firmly at the helm showing us the way. I remember him telling us about a ship he saw docked in a port and how they were cleaning it up, scraping away the mess of shells that was stuck to the hull before it set out on its next voyage. It occurred to him, he said, that what they were doing was an apt way to approach a poem. We needed, he explained, to sweep away the barnacles, the fixed convictions and the blinkered beliefs that dulled the hull of our wonder, before we voyaged out on the ocean of a poem. If we could get into that unburdened, buoyant state of mind, he claimed, we would meet not only the poem but life itself anew each day. An alert readiness to the text of the poem, to the lessons of life; that, he enthused, was the key to knowledge, the way to wellbeing. The idea of being open to the unexpected, alert and attentive to the immediate, appealed to me.

"A sense of wonder at the world" was how Mr Lally summed up this notion of openness. He would take us sometimes on a walkabout around the grounds of the school, getting us to register in our notebooks one significant detail of what we saw.

"In Irish, the word 'file', poet, means to see. Open up your eyes, boys," he urged us. *"Be seers."*

I enjoyed noting down these momentary glimpses.

"I couldn't think of anything to see" was how one boy responded to the exercise.

Mr Lally laughed and complimented him on his wordplay. *"Don't think"* he encouraged the boy. *"Just look!"*

It certainly made me look at things, see connections, have pithy insights. *"On the tip of a bough, a wee thrush made notes for me.*" That's typical of the kind of observation I jotted down while out on these 'Openings' as he called the exercise.

Mr Lally gave us challenging topics to write about, and willed us on to be creative. Once, while studying Emily Dickinson's strange, unsettling poem 'l Felt a Funeral, in My Brain', he brought a small catalogue of surrealist art into the class and introduced us to the eerie, time-warped visions of Dali. He then asked us to imagine that these two were married and living by the sea in Dunfanaghy. 'Miss Dickinson and Mr Dali in Dunfanaghy' was the title he gave us for our homework. It elicited a short poem from me which he praised to the sky.

> My husband dozes
> Somewhere on the horizon
>
> A surrealist catalogue
> Under his head
>
> With a snore
> He breaks the duck-egg of dawn
>
> He dreams of a landscape
> Of broken watches
>
> A breakfast full
> Of time gone nuts
>
> Well for him, no funeral
> Passes through his guts.

I was beginning on my journey to words; a journey I had to make on my own, but Mr Lally was preparing me for it, mapping out as best he could the territory through which I was to travel.

***

One day Mr Lally suggested that I try my hand at writing in Irish. I was in fourth year at the time. It never occurred to me to write in my native language. For many it was, of course, an object of ridicule, the oafish tongue of the bogs, a language of backwardness. I must have been picking up on this; getting the impression that Irish was a spent force, belonging to another time, another place, and maybe even believing a little of it.

English was, by far, my preferred mode of writing. At the time I was reading a lot, voyaging by diving into the floodwaters of a book and coming up worlds away. These transports of joy were entirely in English. My three favourite books that year were Mark Twain's *Huckleberry Finn*, Hermann Hesse's *Narcissus and Goldmund* and Jack Kerouac's *On the Road*. On sleepless nights they kept me company and indeed made me, more often than not, a much-contented insomniac. I was so enthralled by English that I hardly gave a thought to Irish until that fateful day when Mr Lally asked me to write a poem for a local talent competition. As it happened, I won and that whetted my appetite to explore what kind of poetry was being written in Irish. The tech had no library to talk about, only a glass case crammed with a random mix of titles. It did, however, have volumes by the three most noted Irish-language poets of the time.

Seán Ó Ríordáin was the first of these poets to grab my attention. A TB outcast who, during the 1940s, spent long periods in a sanatorium, wrote authentic poems of suffering and self-doubt; poems that grope in the dark, hoping for a foothold on the slippery slopes of uncertainty. And yet, despite the despair so evident in many of them, they are declarations of survival; lighted candles, as it were, in a night of gusting dark. The way that he scrutinises himself, the introspective journeys into his own interior, were so strongly evoked that I felt sometimes as though I was being smothered. Discovering a writer in Irish who, like Gerard Manley Hopkins and Emily Dickinson, was engaged in saying the un-sayable was a hugely exciting find for me. He was an activator of language, a pusher of it. He made it get up and go. Rather than letting Irish speak through him, he forcibly spoke through Irish. The given language was often inadequate for his needs. The risky business of self-scrutiny forced him to shape a language all of his own. It was stimulating to read him from that point of view, to encounter an exciting, individualist expressiveness which was so utterly new to me in Irish. As a teenager, starting off on the quest for my unknown self, these poems, with their tremblings, their loathings, their terrors, spoke directly to my own uncertainties. *Eireaball Spideoige* (A Robin's Tail), Seán Ó Ríordáin's first collection, published in 1952, was the volume that alerted me to his genius. Whoever had it before me had left greased thumbprints and yellowed tea-stains all over the book. They must have kept it in a damp place because a moist, mildewed odour came off it. Whenever I read a poem I got this sick, breathy reek as if it were coughing up its lungs in my face. That made the anguish of his TB-infested sensibilities a terrifyingly real experience for me.

Máire Mhac an tSaoi's collection, *Margadh na Saoire*, was another revelation to me. On the cover it had a delicately beautiful line drawing of a courtly lady reclining on a stylish love seat. The whole look of the book beguiled me; its shape, paper and typeface made me want to hold it, read it. The poems them-selves reminded me of traditional songs, but they were infused somehow with a modern sensibility. However much they were steeped in the past, they spoke of the present. It was Irish singing itself confidently into the twentieth century. It was that music that got me, the vowel harmonies that flowed clear and smooth. The poems existed in the Irish language, it seemed to me, as pure sound, as speech purified, cadenced, charged.

Máirtín Ó Direáin's slim volume of selected poems, *Rogha Dánta*, was an instant hit with me. From Inis Mór, the largest of the Aran Islands, he wrote poems that ennobled the hard struggle of his people with the land, the sea and the elements; a fierce and valiant battle that was in sharp contrast to the grey tedium of his own life as an office worker in the city. He laments an ancient way of life that is passing, with its caring, communal values, and makes plain that he is ill at ease with the self-absorbed society that is taking its place. That grieving nostalgia for a vanished past, for the lost domain of his youth, was beautifully captured in poems that were as sculpted as the faces of his islanders. Out of a bare, pared-down speech, he achieved a haunting, elemental energy that leapt off the page and caught me by the scruff of my senses. If I ever wrote poems in Irish, this approach, I thought, would be what I'd want; a fluid, flexible line that had at times the give of a good fishing-rod and at other times the stretched firmness of a fiddlestring.

Despite the lift I got from these bold, groundbreakingly modern volumes of poetry in Irish, I was still convinced that English would one day be my chosen vehicle of expression.

In my spare time I was writing: love poems, mostly, to those boys who excited me. So as to conceal my true feelings, these poems pretended to be about something else—a standing stone, for instance, or a hillside sapling.

> I want to see your limbs tremble with light
> When the earth moans in your roots;
> I want to see the sap shudder in your trunk
> When the sun tongues your tip;
> I want to see the Spring in you
> As you burst out in shoots of joy.

My poems of that time reeked of teenage lust, and in writing them I was trying to course all those gushing hormones into a spillway of words, which, instead of easing the pressure, left me dizzily unbalanced and convulsed more than ever, with a raring-to-go randiness. It was the first time I had begun to look into that terrible pool of the self. At times like that, you realise you're an abyss, a pitch-black pit. There's only a deep darkness. I got dizzy looking down into the gulf, the chasm of myself. I realised that there was an awful deadening silence . . . That there were no answers. A poem became for me an act of defiance thrown in the face of that silence.

It was also becoming clear to me that, in poetry, naming one's own private unbearable pain was not enough. You had to distance yourself from it; step back and shape it so that the purely personal experience becomes changed into a communal one. This, I was discovering, required real artistry, an imaginative negotiation with words, form and emotion. In class, we were studying Yeats and Eliot. They had it in abundance, that refined amplitude of style that was sadly lacking in my own banal attempts at poems.

I would have shown them to Mr Lally, but something in me feared they were not up to scratch, and I didn't want to bother him with my teenage trivia, my poetry of pimples. Then one day, glancing through a news magazine at school, I came across a snippet about Somerset Maugham which certainly held me back from showing my work too soon.

In the heyday of his literary fame, Maugham often received unsolicited manuscripts from aspiring writers who wanted his blessing on their work. One of these, a young, ambitious novelist who had sent him a voluminous typescript, ran into the great writer in London and with enormous self-importance asked him, *"Should I put more fire into my work?"* Maugham looked him right in the eye and told him bluntly, *"No! Vice versa."* That story brought me to my senses about writing. A lot had to be discarded, I sensed, before you wrote anything of lasting value.

***

At the time, I was struggling to come up with a definition of poetry that satisfied my own need for clarity and at the same time caught something of its inexpressible elusiveness; a liberating explanation that would elucidate rather than ensnare. As fate would have it, I stumbled upon it in a history book. It was just a footnote, an aside to a more pressing narrative. It concerned Lord Norbury*, an eighteenth-century Dublin judge, a hard, exacting man with a wicked sense of humour. Once, while sentencing a man to death for stealing a precious gold watch, he quipped, *"You made a grab at time, idiot, but you caught eternity."* A draconian measure for such a petty crime, however, that phrase, that sentence could be appropriated in a more positive manner to define poetry.

* John 'The Hanging Judge' Toler, otherwise known as the 1st Earl of Norbury, tried Robhert Emmet and sentenced him to death in 1803.

Finding that story was a sweet moment of discovery for me. Finally, I had something that allowed me to catch what was up to then bafflingly evasive. It was a profoundly simple idea. Poetry makes a grasp at time but catches eternity. That means that in spite of the shifting nature of time, poetry manages to grab moments of passing recognition, reveal and illuminate them so that they are captured forever.

In order to do that, I also recognised that a poet had to cultivate what Mr Lally called "*a clear-sighted attentiveness*" in himself. If only I could do to things what the light did to them, I would become a genuine poet, a visionary of the real. I was enthralled by the sudden shifts of light that occur in our hilly climate. Suddenly a hill lights up mysteriously mauve or a field glows in an amber mist or a sunset flush brightens up the face of a gloomy swamp. I wished to make poems that glowed with that light.

Queer Times

I have never been in the closet. I say that because we never had anything as fashionably snazzy as a closet in our house. It's more likely that I was in the *lios*, the abode of the fairies. By sixteen, I came to accept that I was gay. It was an unspoken under-standing with myself. It wasn't the Holy Spirit flaring up in me in a Pentecostal bringing to light; no, it was simply that I had a chance encounter with a book. Literature lured me out of the *lios*.

It was Gore Vidal's *The City and the Pillar*, which my father picked up at random in Glasgow and brought in the big sack of books which he always carried back to me. At the time, it was a godsend, an un-looked-for testament of hope and promise. It was the first time I had read about a romance between two men in a book, and, although their relationship was a tortured one, frightened and doomed to failure, it was an acknowledgement of the public reality of homosexuality. For me, a young adolescent in the wilds of Donegal, coming to terms with my sexual difference, it was an assurance, a guarantee even, that I wasn't on my own. Out there, somewhere, were others of a similar bent. That gave me a mighty shot of self-confidence and cockiness. My falling in love with boys rather than with girls was, I realised, nothing more than a biological predilection. A*bum*inable I may be, it occurred to me at the time, but not abominable.

It was then that I started in earnest to look out for, and read, authors who confessed their gayness in their writings. There were hardly any bookshops in Donegal and certainly none that catered for my particular needs. I had to look elsewhere. The summer before I sat for my Leaving Certificate I worked in a north Dublin hotel and the following summer, soon after finishing exams, I got a job in a hotel in County Wicklow, an hour or so by bus from Dublin. This allowed me to trawl the city-centre bookstores: Webb's, Parsons, the Eblana, Greene's, and find and pleasure myself with Oscar Wilde's *The Picture of Dorian Grey*, Christopher Isherwood's *Goodbye to Berlin*, André Gide's *The Immoralist*, James Baldwin's *Giovanni's Room* and the poetry of Walt Whitman. By putting together this bookish Who's Who of homos, I felt I was being initiated into a gay fraternity of literature. Walt Whitman vowed that he would plant male friendships thick as trees along the riverbanks of America. I knew that he was talking to me directly when he said:

> I mind once how we lay such a transparent summer morning
> How you settled your head athwart my hips
> And gently turned over upon me
> And parted the shirt from my bosom bone
> And placed your tongue to my bare stripped heart
> And reached till you felt my beard
> And reached till you held my feet

That poem was a mighty assuring yes to my condition. At a local charity sale, I came across a copy of Tennessee Williams' *The Glass Menagerie* and bought it. *"What is straight?"* a character asks and the response is, *"A line can be straight, or a street, but the human heart, oh no! It curves like a road through mountains."* I understood that perfectly. The Donegal mountain roads were quite bent.

The Catholicism that I got at primary school was dour and dark; sex was serpent-energy, where the devil inserted his horn into my dick and made it sinfully rigid. If I touched it I was fondling the devil. One day in my final year, a schoolmate told me that he had had a strange experience the night before. He'd rubbed his dick too roughly and the devil had spat at him. He enjoyed it, he said, but was terribly frightened because he must have hurt and angered the devil with his rough handling. I reassured him that anything that hurt the devil was good, positively good. I then suggested that we would hurt the devil together.

And we did. Over the next few weeks, we walloped the devil every chance we got, so much so that he could barely spit in the end. We became deft hands at the emissionary position, that is, until my friend told me rather brusquely that he would much prefer to have a girl share the experience rather than me.

I was lucky in the sense that my mother's faith in the fairy world had a stronger formative and shaping effect on me than Catholicism ever had. After all, I became a 'fairy' myself.

As a young child, I was awe-struck by the grandeur and the solemnity of certain Catholic ceremonies: the Midnight Mass; the Benedictions; the funeral services. The colourful vestments left me gaping, the smell of incense had me in a swoon. Later, as a teenager at the tech, I became appalled at the dogma, the unyielding, harsh canonical tenets that tried to instil in me a terrible sense of shame and guilt about who and what I was. If I fell prey to guilt, I knew that they could easily control me. So I didn't. Love for my fellow men was, I discovered, a pleasure too keen to forgo even with the promise of paradise. Anyway, paradise, as I saw it, was not a place but a position: being joined at the loins with another boy, in joy. I was not going to be branded. I was not going to be confused by labels. Religion, I realised, was extremely wily at making a ceremony of death out of the miracle of life.

A friend of mine told me a joke at the time about a man who couldn't stop wanking. This sinful activity worried him so much that he decided to go to the local priest, a grave, elderly man of great piousness, to get his advice and counsel. Was it acceptable, he asked the priest, to masturbate while he was praying? The old wise priest frowned and told him that it wasn't — but he paused, reflected and then added, *"It's wickedly sinful to masturbate while you are praying but it might be less so if you tried to pray while you masturbated."* The joke beautifully illustrated the fact that you could transgress if only you knew the right theological loophole. That was a heartening realisation.

Anyway, I was getting high on expansiveness be it in pop or in poetry. I was into the bliss business of Eastern beliefs. Karma appealed to me more than dogma.

After all, it was the sixties and I was getting an earful of its vibrations from the radio. Musically, I was weaned on Radio Luxembourg. In the evenings, I would nuzzle up to our little transistor and let that fantastic ferment of sixties sounds flow through me. This music provided the soundtrack to my sexual awakening. Songs like Amen Corner's 'Bend Me, Shape Me', Dusty Springfield's 'I Don't Know What to Do with Myself', Herman's Hermits' 'I'm into Something Good', Steppenwolf's 'Born to be Wild', Manfred Mann's 'Doo Wah Diddy Diddy', The Kinks' 'Lola', The Equals' 'Baby Come Back' and

Procol Harum's 'A Whiter Shade of Pale' were, for me, sexual liberation songs. The Top Twenty was more pertinent to my salvation than the Ten Commandments.

In the early sixties, John Charles McQuaid, the then dourly conservative archbishop of Dublin, stated after returning from a Vatican Two meeting, *"There has been much talk of change. Let me reassure you that no change will disturb the tranquillity of your Catholic lives."* As a stern establishmentarian of the old order, he opposed the radical shake-up of the Church proposed by that progressive Council. Despite the reactionary rhetoric of McQuaid and his ilk, the country was loosening up. The miniskirt saw to that. As hemlines were being raised, sexual scruples were slackening.

De Valera's rural Arcadia, that dreary monochrome ideal of comely maidens and stalwart youths dancing at the crossroads, was gone. A lounge bar permissiveness was taking the place of the dry parish hall dances. The showbands were in full swing. The encouragingly bright economic policies of Lemass were giving the Ireland of the mid-sixties a little bit of technicolour vibrancy.

There was a noticeable burgeoning of prosperity in our area, not so much from any local boom, but from the money earned on well-paid building sites in England and Scotland. People were beginning to rig out their homes with electrical modcons, cookers and kettles, fridges and toasters. Piped water and indoor loos were the in thing.

My father, when he went to Scotland, no longer worked on the farms but stayed with Auntie Biddy in Ballater Street and laboured on roadworks and building sites in Glasgow. With the money he made, we replastered the house, replaced the windows and repaired the roof. An ostentatious 'kitchen cabinet' with sliding glass doors and a wee pull-out table dislodged the dresser. The wide open hearth gave way to a built-up, raised iron grate. However, unlike many of the older houses, where the walls were glossed up with 'beauty board and the flagstones were clad with linoleum', we still limewashed our walls and left our flagstones uncovered.

We drew our own water from the well, still used the outside lavatory and had no television. But we had books, heaps of them, thanks to my father who bought them second-hand in Glasgow and always came home loaded with two or three sacks crammed with a mix of titles. His random pickings allowed me to read about life in the city states of ancient Greece, the fall of the Roman Empire, the Crusades, Buddhism and the path to enlightenment, the pygmies of the Congo jungle, the War of the Roses, the Reformation in Europe, wild flowers of the British Isles and the Hopi Indians and their beliefs. Thomas Hood, Francis Thompson, Walter de la Mare, Edith Sitwell, Wilfred Owen, Vachel Lindsay, Ezra Pound, Robert Service, W.H. Auden,

William Wordsworth, John Keats, Edward Thomas were the poets that he brought to me. The list of fiction is too long to enumerate but included authors like John Steinbeck, Ernest Hemingway, Boris Pasternak, Compton McKenzie, Zane Grey, Lewis Carroll, Gore Vidal, E.M. Forster, Hermann Hesse, Jack Kerouac and Mark Twain.

These books raised me out of rural isolation and allowed me to enter multiple worlds of experience, thus broadening my mind to other cultures, to other valid and varied ways of seeing and thinking about the world I lived in.

At the tech, Mr Lally, a great encourager of ideas and a disseminator of them too, would give over a class entirely to debate; an open forum for free thinking on a wide range of topics. Should we legalise contraception, allow divorce, decriminalise homosexuality, abandon religion, adopt socialism? Should there be women priests? We discussed mini-skirts and Women's Lib, unmarried mothers, censorship, the Cold War and a whole lot of other current social issues.

He introduced us to the psychedelic concepts of love-ins and be-ing and all the tuned-in buzz words of that hallucinogenic decade: dope, turned on, trip, stoned, high, spaced out. We wrote essays on 'Flower Power', 'Does Free Love Really Free Us Up', 'Jesus Was the First Hippy', 'The Idea of a Commune'. He tried to inculcate in us a sense of the liberating times that we lived in so that we would be better equipped to benefit from them. Fortunately for him and for us, the tech was not under the oppressive thumb of the Church. If it had been, the liberal bountifulness of his teaching would not have been tolerated. In this truly secular space, Mr Lally created a free zone of thinking—a bold, Haight-Ashbury of our own in the Bay Area of Gortahork—that gave me and my classmates much latitude to develop.

In my final year at the tech, I wrote a batch of poems in Irish inspired by Michael Davitt and Gabriel Rosenstock, two young contemporary poets whose work was causing a bit of a stir in the Irish-language literary world. One of these poems, 'Bóitheach na Bó', would be my first bit of published writing.

Michael Davitt was a child of the sixties, a free-wheelin' follower of the new vision, a believer in that costumed counter-culture that put a rosy glow in the mind and a rainbow show in the wardrobe. He took me out in the carefree caravan of his poetry to a lovely mellow yellow domain somewhere between Dylan and Dún Chaoin.

Likewise, the poetry of Gabriel Rosenstock was dashingly cool and daringly hip. Their dialogue with other cultures, their impish humour, their openness to the unexpected made his poems hugely appealing. I had found my role models.

CEREMONY

On this altar, this bed,
I celebrate your body
with my ritual desire.
Every graceful, virginal limb—
I bow humbly before them
and with kisses for prayers,
I fervently adore
every muscle and sinew
as a choir of senses sing
a jubilant hymn to your virtues—
your mouth, midriff and chest—
that fiery trinity of delight.
And as the ceremony gathers
intensity and momentum,
I tremble inside, waiting
for the joyful miracle.
And it'll come, come pouring
when I've unlocked your mystery,
your manhood—that chalice
of desire. It will come,
the joy of joys,
as a sacrament, an offering,
in fiery tongues of knowledge.
An intimation of heaven
will come.

—*Translated by Frank Sewell*

SCARS

Dearest love, I think of you always,
your strong arms, *your politesse*,
your soft kisses.

We will last as long as life itself,
you said. And when you left,
you cut my soul to the quick.

If I come back in another lifetime,
it will be to forget you
for once and for all.

—Translated by Frank Sewell

A LOVE SONG SURROUNDED BY SLAUGHTER

While we were making out,
making a song and dance of life
on the reed of our love,
as the Persian poets used to say,
war was raging, plague spreading
and famine feeding on flesh.
People like us, gay lovers,
were being targeted, many of us
battered and brutalized in prison.

While we were making out,
women were raped, children abused,
free thinkers locked in jails,
violence advocated in the name of God,
forests felled, rivers polluted
and somewhere deep in the universe
a star exploded as we
tangled in each other's arms.

But we kept on making out,
making a song and dance of life
on the reed of our love,
as the Persian poets used to say.

—Translated by Frank Sewell

NIGHT

It wasn't much of a room
one of those B&Bs off Gardiner Street
damp on the walls   the sheets yellow with grime
nothing to listen to but the slow moan
of the drunkening city and the racket
from bin-hoking cats in the yard   but so what?
weren't you lying flat on your back on the edge
of the bed   undressed to the nines?

and you clung to me so tight   your laugh trans-
forming the dirty room and murky night outside
to bliss   there on the wreck of a bed you
in all your pow and glory   my quiet young lover
there on that hard hurting bed with stale
sweat rising from the damp sheet   your warm
comforting lips kissed my blood alight

that night   I could do anything with your slender
smooth body   your belly bright as a foaming wave
and below   more tempting than autumn apples
in store   mine were the rolling drumlins of your cheeks
soft under my hand and light as the scantiest silk
now   alone   on a no-such-lucky bed   in pain
in joy   I remember you   beautiful   naked

transforming my night   eighteen years ago   tonight

—*Translated by Frank Sewell*

197

4. A Spell in Delhi

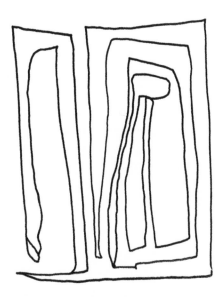

1

Damp overcast skies all week. The air is a thick broth of fog. It leaves me queasy. My lungs wheeze as I cough up a black, moist sludge.

Delhi is one of the worst polluted cities in the world, its air as life threatening as its traffic. A foul, metallic tang hangs on the air, the nasty reek of belching traffic.

Everywhere the traffic lanes are clogged with the thick volume of vehicles passing through. The long, weary tailbacks, the unbearable bottlenecks, the tortuous congestions make driving in Delhi a real ordeal.

Although I'm not a driver myself and never had the urge to be one—I can empathize with those disgruntled drivers who get themselves into a high-octane road rage. The stress of navigating Delhi's roadways would test anyone's attempt at restraint and composure. The city needs a whole new traffic management action plan to ensure a smoother and less taxing vehicular flow.

Weaving one's way through this daily snarl is hazardous.

I ask myself why do I stay here in this inferno with its suffocating reek of exhausts, its stink and its clatter. Why subject myself to the mutter and groan of ongoing traffic, the sonic boom of backfiring motor-bikes, the blare and peal of horns.

I put it down to familiarity, the assurance of a place that I know; where to stay, where to go, where to eat and more importantly where I'm friendly with some locals.

A guarantee of familiarity and a need to be grounded! How different to the past when it was only the uncharted that called and charmed me, the *terra incognita* of a far-off mountain village, the breath-taking frontier of a high altitude path. That was a time when I was tempted by risk and driven by the rash. I always wanted to be out there in the stark; where the random, the unfamiliar and the raw took hold of me and filled me with daring.

That desperate ache to take the headlong leap in the dark was for years what drove me on into the unknown.

But age has tamed those prodigal impulses, chastened that bold, wanton recklessness. I have not, I hope, lost that appeal for the unforeseen but I have become more cautious in my approach to it.

The lure of the habitual and the hold of habit-forming can lead to stagnation. I have to avoid that. The challenge is to know when to go out on a limb and when to stay put in one's own comfort zone.

2

I'm staying at the Hari Piorko Hotel, one of the better lodgings of the Paharganj area, a place full of cheap, shoddy backpackers' hotels. Many of these rundown dumps boast such grandiose names as 'Grand Palace', 'Hotel Sun Deluxe International', 'Hotel Oasis Delight'. Many, like the 'Sky View Super Deluxe' are buried away in tight, gloomy alleyways where you hardly get a glint of daylight.

Grim, airless rooms with soiled linen and broken fixtures. In 2013 during my stay here, I moved into one of these cheerless dives to cut costs. Being entombed in that soulless room for two weeks was a ghastly experience. It looked fine when I first saw it and I went ahead and paid up for the duration of my stay. That was short-sighted of me. I had no option then but to stay. I couldn't afford an alternative place.

Whenever I turned on the tap in the hand basin it rasped and coughed out a few noxious dribbles. The shower fared no better. I resorted to washing myself with bottled water. I like a hotel room where I can relax, drink tea, write. This drab, stale, arid place was conducive to none of these things.

The nights were a slow, weary drag in that airless room, as if Time itself had lost its resolve. A little clock that I kept with me for many years on my travels and that chirped cheerily by my bedside conked out and could not be revived. It was a bad omen. Day and night that little clock passed the time by keeping its hands busy and it was for me, tending towards indolence as I do, a lesson in diligence, steadfastness, rigour and clarity.

When I complained about the lack of water; the foul-smelling reek from the toilet; the deadly hissing and sparking of the fluorescent tubing on the ceiling; the manager, an elderly, plump, greying man with a fox-red tint in his hair, came to inspect and assured me that the last guest, a Romanian pastry chef was more than happy *"in this lovely sweet room."*

As he was leaving he appraised himself in the gaudy, slightly tarnished, oval mirror on the wall and said *"beautiful mirror"* with unbiased approval and looking at me with a blameless grin, *"and it works. Take a look."* And he left.

And I did. I looked at myself in that mirror and laughed out loud at my own smug, self-indulgent notions of comfort. It raised my spirits.

This time I made sure I got a room that is to my satisfaction. It is a spacious, bright, elegantly-furnished, marble-floored bedroom with a good sized attached bathroom. Everything in it is chosen with a genteel tact; the graceful writing desk, the carved wood units by the bed, the gleaming mirror that takes up one entire wall, the two brown, pinstriped easy arm-chairs and a black, leather-bound, straight-back chair. It even has a built-in aquarium by the door which gives me hours of calm, soothing viewing, the kind of mental repose that I never get from watch-ing television.

The only quibble I have is that it has no access to natural light. It makes up for it, though, in its bright, well-lit ambience; the mirror accentuating the light and, as it were, highlighting it so that the room glows with a luminous warmth.

It is a place of grace and peace where I get a great sense of well-being and composure. I'm happy to ease away the hours here, reading, writing, drinking tea, viewing the scintillating lives in the fish tank.

The staff are well trained in strict hotel etiquette. Attentive, friendly, refined, they do their duties with decorum and a sparkling smile. It is not the kind of sickening obeisance that is common in India but a natural courtesy, a lovely propriety and politeness that puts guests at ease.

The menu is varied with a whole range of tasty Asian and European foods available. It's multicultural cuisine for a pittance.

From Paharganj it's a ten-minute walk along the faded grandeur of Chelmsford Road to Connaught Place, the circular, neoclassical, colonnaded city centre, a place full of designer chic emporia, westernized coffee bars, nightspots and milling crowds. Most days on my walkabouts I go there for a shot of good coffee and to browse in the bookshops. There are also many pavement booksellers dealing in a wide range of cheap paperbacks.

3

Everywhere in Delhi you can see the monumental sprawl of its past, the imperial domed settings of Mughal pomp, the lofty magnificence of Hindu and Sikh temples, the fading neo-classical grandeur of British dominion.

Nowadays, the rose sandstone forts of the Muslim dynasties and the bougainvillea bungalows of the

Raj are interspersed with the high-rise commercialism of modern Delhi.

It is a city strewn with the heavy debris of the past dragging itself into a tired, misshapen modernity. And yet, I love it for all its incongruities; its vulgar voguishness; its swagger; its scamsters. It intrigues me. It irritates me. It inspires me.

This capital of a secular democracy is a complex and sensitive place with its Quranic madrasas, its Hindu devotional sects, its evangelical proselytisers.

How to accommodate fundamentalist mindsets be they Muslim ideologues or Hindu triumphalists; how to get sects, castes, linguistic communities to cohabit rather than to confront each other. Delhi is a bazaar of religious lifestyles— Hindu, Sikh, Muslim, Jain, Buddhist, Christian, all adding their own devout colours, their vigorous, unyielding beliefs to the thorny project of a democratic India committed to secularism.

Hanging around cafés, and dealing with shopkeepers, tailors, rickshaw drivers, I hear whispers of disquiet and rumours of discord and resentment. The emboldened bigots of all religions are incensed by this worldly state of affairs and want to impose their own brand of divine will on the populace.

Delhi down through the ages and indeed into our own times has gone through periodic cycles of mass violence, brutal struggles and sectarian carnage.

In 1398 Tamerlane and his Mongolian hordes ransacked the city and slew much of its people. Babur the Muslim conqueror occupied Delhi in 1526 and so began the imperial Mughal reign. In 1803 the British captured the city and in 1911 it replaced Calcutta as their capital and became the hub of a bureaucratic elite especially after it was radically refashioned in the 1920s by Lutyens. Since independence in 1948 it has retained that power and prestige.

It's also a great outlet for all kinds of sham spirituality. The wayout, the bogus, the wacky is on offer for the unsuspecting seeker.

You can have a Pranic retreat, a psycho detox, a week of nurturing your bio-sensors or a month of Vedantic lovetrance.

You can learn how to vibrate your molecules with Sanskrit chants; you can bliss up your chi and heal your chakras with a tantric massage.

You can also fork out a lot of money to participate in a divine course of god-intoxication at a new age ashram.

And if you don't have a sufficiently powerful transcendental experience in Delhi you can always move on to Rishikesh or Tamil Nadu for more of the same, at a price, of course! Enlightenment for many is merely going home with a lighter pocket. But Delhi is not all about lovey-dovey beads and bells or incense-burning ayurvedic ministrations or meditative raptures at the manicured feet of some venerated Guru.

When you get out and about, a more sombre reality sinks in and shocks you. The disparity between the privileged classes in their showy mansions and the aggrieved poor in their slum colonies is enormous. Even a cursory outing around the city will alert you to the opulent lifestyles of the monied and the pitiable conditions of the kerb dwellers and the gutter pickers.

It is a real challenge for policy makers to address and remedy this huge social imbalance. As I write this Narendra Modi of the BJP party is urging the populace to become active citizenry in what he promises to be a participatory democracy if he is elected.

His maxim of *"minimum government, maximum governance"* has a mass appeal for the *'aam aadmi'*, the common man who is fed up and furious with the corruption, the greed, the bullying tactics of officialdom.

I get the impression that Modi's politico-speak is more than ideological bravado, more than a succinct electoral strategy to mobilize the people. I believe that he genuinely wants to better society.

However, I detect a strong Hindu nationalism coming from his BJP party. This is worrying for the populous Muslim minority in India. Modi has to allay their fears, otherwise those deep-seated religious and ethnic divisions will come to the fore again in grim blood-letting.

Taking the bribery, the profiteering, the crookedness out of the civil administration would be a good start. Reducing the hassle and the red tape that one encounters when dealing with public officials would enhance the system and the lives of its citizens.

4

I spend a lot of my time in the leafy, spaciously peaceful Lodi Gardens close to the Khan Market in central Delhi.

I usually hire an auto-rickshaw to get there. Although I have a Smartcard for the Metro and it's a fraction of the cost of an auto-rickshaw, the press and crush of people is usually too much to bear and I take the more expensive but less stressful option.

On the Metro I have to change three times to get to Khan Market. From R.K Ashram to Rajiv Chowk, from there to Central Secretariat and then onwards to Khan Market.

It is a very cheap, efficient underground system, splayed out all over Delhi. The volume of people who use it is huge. And that means over-crowded, tightly packed, stuffy carriages. Rajiv Chowk is usually a seething, living hell of jostling people rushing from one line to another.

This feverish stir, the scramble and scurry of commuters leave me whacked, weary and gasping for an exit.

There doesn't seem to be a fixed number of passengers to a carriage or else nobody pays any attention to numerical restrictions. It's just push and shove and pile in until it's crammed and not an inch to spare. I hate that rammed-in, squeezed helplessness as we hurtle headlong through the dark, stale underworld. One could easily lose one's head and rave hysterically in this airless confinement. I have to restrain myself, close my eyes, breathe deeply and forbear.

It's lovely to be out in the leisured, unhurried ease of the Lodi Gardens, sprawled on the warm grass or lounging on a shady seat.

It has a number of monumental tombs; grand architectural edifices housing the royal dead. One of these is the splendid tomb of Muhammad Shah Sayyid who ruled 1434–44, and belonged to the Sayyid Dynasty of Sultans which reigned for a short period (1414–51). It has an octagonal shape, beautifully corbelled doorways, a decorative plaster finish and a colonnaded walkway. It is surrounded on all sides by a row of tall, shapely, silver trees that remind me of Doric columns. Their tag names them

Roystonea Regia and they are regally beautiful, grandly statuesque trees with very discernible rings and a crown of frond-like leaves at the very top.

There is also the imposing Bara Gumbad Mosque erected during the Lodi period (1451–1526), another Sultanate. Built with grey quartzite stone and a mixture of red sandstone in the doorways to relieve monotony, it is a big domed building, beautiful in its pleasing proportions and rich in arabesque stucco decorations of floral and geometrical designs.

While I was there today, a pair of eager lovers in a corner were trying to snatch come furtive kisses without being seen. I could sense a hot-blooded tryst and the social strictures against such sensuous public displays of affection only added, I'm sure, to their amourous excitements.

It's lovely to compose oneself under an ancient, gnarled peepal tree (*figus infectoria*) and listen to the gregarious screeches of the green parakeets and the more sedate call of the bulbuls—a black-crested bird with brownish upper parts, scalloped with white—or catch a glimpse of a golden-back wood-pecker with his huge dagger-like bill and brilliant red forehead and crest. There are blue rock pigeons in flight above me and house swifts pecking among the flower beds.

5

Penguin India are in the news nowadays because they have withdrawn and pulped *The Hindus—An Alternative History* by American scholar Wendy Doniger. The have capitulated to the demands of a fanatical Hindu group which disapproves of the book. Many Indian writers are dismayed at Penguin's regrettable stance on the crucial issue of free speech. Why have they not stood their ground and shown some courage in the face of such bigoted intimidation?

It shows how afraid they are of offending religious fundamentalists. They are fearful about the consequences of defying these hardline radicals. Of course, this yielding to their warped, fanatical demands only emboldens their intolerant agenda.

The upholding of free expression is enshrined in the Indian Constitution but the political establishment does not show a proper commitment to that ideal.

We have seen what happens when ideology becomes a hardened illiberal absolute.

On 10 May 1933, 25000 books were burned in Berlin because they were considered un-Germanic.

As a result of the formation of the House of Un-American Activities Committee in 1938 any artist who was suspected of communist sympathies was blacklisted.

The Stalinist regime in the old USSR was notorious for the arrest, exile and even execution of free thinkers.

And in Ireland we had our own book purges instigated by the Church who did not approve of intellectual freedom and together with the State apparatus concocted a narrow, unabashedly purist notion of Irishness and a sanitized version of our culture.

We have seen how a repressive religious ideology hounded Salman Rushdie and also less well-known authors like the Bangladeshi novelist Taslima Nasreen who was accused of un-Islamic sentiment in her work and had to seek refuge abroad.

Likewise, Maqbool Fida Husain, one of India's most revered painters had his work vandalized and had to flee his homeland due to religious extremism.

It must be depressing for Indian authors to have this sort of intellectual censure imposed upon them by religious bigots. Having to remain deferential and reverential on issues of religious belief, morality and sexuality stifles free speech, thwarts new ideas from coming forth and obstructs the creative imagination.

This interfering, prohibitive hostility to fresh ideas, original thinking and independent outlooks is a real obstacle to those authors who want to challenge preconceived notions of belief and behaviour.

The question must be asked whether in a secular state blasphemy — which is merely a challenge to whatever the prevalent dogma happens to be — should be considered an offence. I lean, myself, towards the idea that all religious hegemony should be challenged.

The present day disapproval in India of any overt display of sexuality is in stark contrast to the graphic, erotic couplings with their contortionist positions and their unfazed, multi-partner licentiousness that are found on ancient temple carvings throughout India. These fleshy pageants of the sensual are an abhorance to the zealots, the narrow-minded, the fanatical.

A time may come when they too are defaced and destroyed. Look at what happened to the beautiful, rock buddhas of Banyan: two thousand years of sacred stone serenity was hacked to bits because of their alien otherness among a brain-washed populace.

It's a small Hindu Right party under the leadership of Dinanath Batra, with its intolerant agenda and its bullying tactics that forced Penguin India to pulp Wendy Doniger's book.

When Batra, a former school principal, talks about "Indianness" in the field of education you know that he has a very narrow vision of modernity. In strong denunciatory rhetoric he castigates the shameless, degenerate, freethinking modern world and insists that education in India should be for the sole purpose of purifying the minds of the young and keeping them free from Western corruption.

Tolerant debate, open-minded discussion, progressive discourse are anathema to Mr Batra's severe, single-minded mind-set.

Wendy Doniger's book is a 600-page tome of exacting scholarly research. I spent a half hour leafing through it in the Full Circle Bookshop in Khan Market and found it a broad, hugely informative volume. I intended to buy it on my next visit to the shop but by then it had been withdrawn.

Today I got talking to a patrician-looking man in a white dhoti who was reading the book in Lodi Gardens. Neeraj was his name but in Canada — where he lived most of his adult life and where he worked successfully in the textile trade — he was commonly known as Neil. Now he and his Indian wife in their retirement divided their time between Toronto and Delhi.

He believed that the book was valid and an important contribution to the history of Hinduism. He was particularly excited by how Doniger explored the role of Dalits and women in the evolution of the Hindu religion and how much of their contribution was expurgated over the centuries by a male priestly caste who wanted to impose their own dry, narrow, purist viewpoint on the narrative.

Doniger bills the book as an alternative history and Neeraj praises it for its fresh, innovative look at the epics, the histories, the texts out of which Hinduism emerged.

It was a very creditable interpretation, he said, and Doniger should be commended for the sheer scholastic scope of the venture.

Meanwhile Dinanath Batra accuses her of "*Christian missionary zeal and a hidden agenda to show Hinduism in a poor light.*"

Freedom of speech and expression, the liberty to raise issues, to hold opinions; the civil right to receive and impart information so that we are an informed citizenry are important factors in a functioning democracy.

Mr Batra and his Hindu Right will have nothing of that, forward-looking outlook. They want to impose their own repressed, domineering, feudal thinking on the population. Like the Taliban, like Isis, like Boko Haram, they want everyone to live unquestioning servitude to their harsh dictates.

6

The big story on the news channels is the gang rape of a young girl in a west Bengal village. A Hindu girl was having a relationship with a Muslim boy and that was not socially acceptable. She had broken the strict, uncompromising code of her tribe and the village elders—men, of course—passed judgement that she should be gang raped in retribution for her sins.

How barbarous! How ungodly to inflict such punishment on an innocent young girl who merely opened her heart to an outsider.

The report states that she was gang raped and that there were 13 men involved in this heinous crime.Honour killings, maimings, acid attacks are commonplace happenings in India.

Women are seen not as individuals but as the property, the chattel of men. Women are commodities and society demands that they be stamped and monetized by the ownership of men.

Every day on my walkabouts, I see how young girls are preyed upon by lewd whistles and sordid remarks and even, sometimes, a blatant fondling of breasts and buttocks.

Sixty odd years ago India threw off the yoke of colonization but still her womenfolk are colonized. Women are still under the sway of an oppressive patriarchy, still in the clutches of a severe feudalism.

Often the police turn a deaf ear to crimes committed against women. The judicial system connives with, and in most cases, upholds male hegemony. Here society is still determined by class, caste and gender.

The constraints of a male custodian culture make it difficult for a woman to break loose, to throw off the burden of servitude. Bollywood blockbusters are often crude, misogynistic narratives that reinforce the values of a patriarchal culture.

You can see that in those song and dance routines that are an integral part of Hindi movies—the sexy, gyrating allure of the female is to depict her as a temptress. It is the role of the male to subdue, master and reform her. It seems to me that when a woman is saying "no" to the advances of a mulish male in one of those movies the impression given is that she is not really saying "no". It is not a very healthy or a wholesome depiction of women.

The *Khap-Panchayats*, the kangaroo courts who pass judgement on moral matters in the villages, operate as severe, stiff, parallel law courts and enforcement agencies and are beyond the dictates of the standard legal system.

They are a repressive, inhibiting authority all over India and are responsible for barbaric punishments. There are at least 1000 reported honour killings in India every year and it is all about the right to choose; custom and community versus individual choice. Love marriages, the right to choose one's partner and especially from another caste is illicit to

a large extent. It's a communal taboo. I think it's be-
cause of the fear that it would throw the whole caste
structure into jeopardy.

7

I'm in the National Museum in Janpath to see the
Harappa and Mohenjo-Daro exhibits.

The Harappa civilisation, also known as the Indus
Valley civilisation was contemporary with the Egypt-
ian, Mesopotamian and Yellow River civilisations.

Its early phase was 3500–2600 BC; its mature phase
2600–2000 BC; its decline 2000–1500 BC.

Although a rather elusive and enigmatic Bronze
Age culture in that we have no recorded accounts
of its history, its people or its places; no name of a
king, a hero, or even a god, and despite the fact that
for millennia it lay without visible trace underneath
sand and silt, the alluvial debris of the ages; yet it
has been possible to construe from its mud and rubble
mounds that it was once a highly developed urban
culture.

This extraordinary culture flourished in the north
western part of the Indian sub-continent in the area
known today as Pakistani Punjab and principally in
the river basins of the Indus and the Sarasvati rivers.
The first site was discovered in 1921 at Harappa and

since then the name has become synonymous with a civilization that extended for a thousand miles from the North to the Arabian Sea and at its peak it was more widespread than its counterparts in Egypt and Mesopotamia.

Excavations, so far, have unearthed more than 4000 sites pertaining to different phases of this ancient culture but the focus has mainly been on the great urban centres of Harappa in the Punjab; Mohenjo-daro, four hundred miles or so further south in Sindh province and Lothal at the south end in Gujarat at the head of the Gulf of Cambay.

Just as the alluvial flood plains of the Nile gave sustenance to the opulent splendours of Egypt and the waters of the Tigris and the Euphrates allowed a great culture to flourish in the Fertile Crescent, so too did the Indus, Saravati and its tributaries support its people and enable them to become a significant cultural zone in the third and second millennia BC.

Today the area is largely rainless and thus arid and infertile. Climate change and the shifting of river courses due to strong tectonic activity was probably one of the prime causes of the demise of this culture around 1500 BC.

Environmental factors and especially the drying-up of water sources and the salination of the soil has led to the collapse of many great civilizations.

From the archaeological discoveries made over the past century in this vast area it seems fair to say that the Harappan culture was a homogenous, largely uniform one.

All of the sites that have been excavated show a similar approach to town planning. They were the first, perhaps, to try out a properly planned urbanscape. Theirs is the earliest trial run in urban habitation.

A regular, grid type layout with well-defined streets, roadways, thoroughfares is evident in all their cities. The Harappan metropolis had a strict, standardised uniformity about it. All of the cities have the exact same pattern: two distinct localities, a citadel in the upper part, built on a big brick platform and occupied by members of a ruling class, perhaps, or a priestly caste, and the lower town with rectangular shaped brick houses of varying sizes; the residential and commercial quarters, housing merchants, artisans, labourers.

The health and cleanliness of its citizenry seems to have been a priority of Harappan governance. Whether they be of the lower orders or of the titled and ranked nobility, everybody seems to have lived in well built, fire-brick houses with good sanitary and sewage amenities. The amount of waste disposal ducts and sewerage systems in all the cities attest to this municipal beneficence.

Unlike Egypt or Mesopotamia, the Harappans did not build enduring monumental edifices. They used small kiln-fired bricks rather than dressed stone and these are not as amenable to long lasting towering structures. This baked clay, this mortar of mud, does not have the ageless durability of stone and is prone of course to the grinding down and the crumbling caused by sun, salt and wind.

There are many gaps in our understanding of this culture, what were their spiritual beliefs, who or what did they worship, what were their rituals, their ceremonies, their devotional customs.

They used earth burials rather than cremations to dispose of their dead. Burial urns have been unearthed.

However, unlike the Egyptians and the Mesopotamians who had a well-fleshed pantheon of deities, we don't know the names of the Harappan gods. It's unlikely that they were a secular culture, unawed and impious. Stone images of the phallus and the vulva were found at Harappa, similar to the lingam/yoni iconography of later Hindu worship.

Terracotta figurines of women were found at all sites. Were they cult images? Fertility goddesses? We are still to find a clear understanding of who their idols were and what were their liturgical observances.

Their ideas of the sacred and their otherworldly beliefs may become clearer when their writing is deciphered. So far, no one has succeeded in unlocking the secrets of their largely pictographic writing system.

They were a hugely developed culture who used the potter's wheel, who had a uniform script, who devised regulated weights and measures, who had highly skilled goldsmiths, weavers of wool and cotton, breadmakers, bronzesmiths; who had carts with solid wheels, who navigated the coast of the Arabian Sea and who had widespread trade and commercial links with Afghanistan, Iran, Central Asia and with the cultures of Egypt and the Mesopotamian basin; who domesticated oxen, goats, sheep, pigs, buffaloes, and, of course, who developed a highly effective mode of urban planning. In most of the city sites so far excavated the largest building is usually a granary. The fertile soil of the enriched and well-irrigated river basins produced wheat, barley, peas, mustard and rice. It is thought that these cereals and food grains were received as taxes from the peasants and stored in these huge granaries as barter for the exchange of goods from elsewhere and as payment for the wages of officials. Seals the size of postage stamps with carved intaglio designs and inscriptions on them, used for stamping goods, are a common find at all of the excavated sites, which goes to show an ordered, highly evolved and structured code of commerce.

In the National Museum there is a wide range of exhibits that show the extraordinary artistry of Harappan craftspeople; the beautiful red ware pottery painted with black designs, the domestic pots, bowls, huge storage jars, the terracotta figurines of humans, animals, birds; the assortment of semi-precious stone necklaces, the toiletries, combs, mirrors, tweezers.

I was enthralled to see the well known and iconic figure from this culture — the finely sculpted miniature bronze, the pocket size 'Dancing Girl' from Mohenjo-daro (circa 2500 BC).

Slim, fine-limbed, naked, alive in her movements and gestures, with a hand on her hip and the other on her knee, her carefully plaited head thrown back, with bangled arms and braceleted neck, she glides effortlessly between ages, a lively dancer who weaves a magical thread between the ancient past and the present.

A beautiful image, sensuously evoked by an unknown artist from the dawn of civilization. So ancient and yet so modern in its conception.

It's as if time past and time future coalesced and fused in this embodiment of harmony and grace. It's an image of the joyous dance of light, the creative spirit that permeates the universe.

There is also a very striking bust of a meditative male figure in white soapstone also from Mohanjo-daro, a serene, otherworldly face gazing across the abyss of the ages.

I am awed at this great, progressive and still mystifying civilization that was for millennia buried in silt and almost lost to memory and at last is slowly coming to light with the skilled expertise of the archaeologist's trowel.

This innovative, productive culture that made huge technological headway; these pioneers of urban planning and the first, maybe, to invent wheeled transport and to mastermind the spinning and weaving of cotton.

They were a Bronze Age culture whose range of tools, knives, sickles, chisels were made from copper, bronze and stone — mostly a quartz-type stone — and yet, theirs were a productive economy with expert agriculturalists, skilled artisans and a thriving land and sea commerce.

And it came to pass that around 1500 BC the drying up and desertification of their lands and settlements caused the decline of the Harappans and so the collapse of one of the most enterprising of the ancient civilizations.

8

For the past three days I'm down with a severe bout of diarrhoea. Delhibelly! I put it down to an infected bowl of chicken and mushroom soup I had at a local café.

Here the digestive tract is under daily threat. A seething mass of bugs is milling around ready to pounce. You have to be vigilant and sensible where you eat and what you eat and, even then, prudence and watchfulness can be undone in a mouthful.

After three days of this runny leakage I feel sapped and fragile and reluctant to go out.

I just lie on the bed and gloat about my condition —bloat about my condition would be more apt— my abdomen, never anything but beefy, is, even more swollen than usual and despite a volatile flatulence shows no sign of decrease.

Initially I took Immodium but it had no effect whatsoever in arresting the slimy deluge that issued from me. At last I had to resort to a course of antibiotics —which I am disinclined to do if it is at all possible to avoid them—but within an hour or two the flow had stopped and I felt a tightening up of my bowels. Lovely to be back to the plop and splash of a normal shite.

I am also getting back an appetite and a taste for food. I'm having a light snack here in the Hari Piorko Rooftop Restaurant; fresh orange juice, a lemon pancake and a pot of jasmine tea.

This is a lovely area of carefully groomed bushes and many potted shrubs and flowering plants. I can still hear the rumble of the street three or four storeys below me but here in this elevated retreat the alarm and noise is muffled and softened by protective greenery.

I'm sitting under an open, thatched-roofed structure supported by four timber poles. It gives me the impression of an exotic beach hut and I'm looking out at an immensity of blue sea-sky.

Actually, the sky has been mostly ashen and cheerless since I got here. An occasional faint blue one appears but is soon veiled in swathes of heavy grey. But today a full-blown, azure-blue sky beams down at us.

At street level it's clammy warm but up here a light breeze freshens the air and perks me up. This rooftop refuge is full of birds. Their swoop and perch and sudden chatter delights me. A sudden flash of blue and green as a small flock of noisy parrots alights on a smartly manicured hedge to my right and just as quickly takes off again; a wonderful aerial display of bright plumage that leaves a lovely spill of colour filling my whole being.

A whistling thrush pipes up to my left, a number of plump, cheeky sparrows settles on my table and pecks at the crumbs I spread out for them. There are many birds that I can't identify but I'm happy to exult in their chants and chatterings and shrill cries.

Pink, pastel-shaded geraniums, big bold, golden marigolds, mauve-coloured convolvulus, yellow jasmine and flaming-red roses flourish up here and enliven the air with a hint of fragrance.

It's lovely to sit here in my thatched pavillion and let this gentle benediction of birdsong, scented verdure and cool air lift my spirits.

9

Today I went to Chandni Chowk, the best known of Delhi's old bazaars. It's a wide, bustling corridor of commerce with numerous offshoots, passage-ways, aisles, back alleys and arcades. Like a lot of old Delhi it's a hodgepodge of crumbling decay and flashy newness; a jostling shantytown of hawkers and hustlers; of sari shops and spice markets; of frying food stalls and roadside cobblers; of porters weighted down with huge bales of cloth, and cruising rick-shaw drivers clamouring for trade.

At its eastern end it boasts the big parapeted splendour of the Red Fort, a 17th-century, palatial magnificence built by Shah Jahan, the same man who built the beautiful Taj Mahal in Agra in memory of his dead wife. During the Mughal dynasty you would probably see showy processions of ceremonial elephants and royal palanquins parading here where now it's the roar and whine of traffic that speeds past.

In Haldiram's, a famed cafeteria that excels in sweets and savouries I meet Amir Khan. Sitting at the same table, we strike up a conversation. He is a twenty year old Muslim from the the state of Bihar, speaks English, albeit haltingly, and is a tailor.

"Do you like cricket?" he asks enthusiastically while we sip our coffee.

A common question. The Indians, despite their deep sectarian divisions, are as one as far as cricket is concerned. Here, a mutual love of the game pervades the masses.

I have no interest whatsoever in cricket, though. Watching a match would be as mindless as watching a down drip from the roof for hours on end on a rainy day. But I'm careful not to be so blunt in case I offend.

"Cricket is great if your country has a good team," I offer rather glibly.

"But Ireland is very good," he replies before singing the praises of the Irish cricket team at length. I nod and listen in awe and astonishment as he lauds my national team and lists their various triumphs. I knew nothing about their success but to show my ignorance of such a worthy team would be uncivil and rude. I smile benignly and thank him for taking such a keen interest in our cricketing prowess.

"What is your religion?" he then asks with a disarming smile.

Another awkward moment. Should I tell him I'm an unbeliever? Devout people find it difficult to countenance the idea of a person being godless.

"I'm from a Christian background," I say without committing myself too much. That seems to satisfy him. I am from an approved orthodoxy.

When we finished our coffee he invited me back to his room. Outside, he laced his fingers through mine and we sauntered along through the busy streets in a lovely, unhurried intimacy.

He lives in a predominantly Muslim area near the Fatehpuri Masjid. I noticed that many of the young men sported beards and that the girls wore the hijab. Amir tells me that the place is often dubbed 'Mini Pakistan'. But these young, devout Muslims, most of them educated and well-adjusted, are also a part of the mainstream, globalized youth and are as conversant with techno-gadgetry as any of their western counterparts. They may not be exactly free-thinking but they are forward-looking.

Amir's room is up two flights of stairs, the living quarters and a workshop in one. His father and two younger brothers sit cross-legged in front of sewing machines when we enter, an array of finished and half-finished menswear garments hanging on a rack behind them; shirts, pants, jackets, waistcoats.

The father, a tall, handsome, midddle-aged man in a grey djellaba, greats me warmly and settles me down on a couch of piled cushions. Soon I'm offered a glass of sweet, aromatic mint tea and a plateful of fancy cakes.

Only Amir speaks English and although he does his best to be a go-between, our conversation is somewhat constrained.

I tell them a little about Ireland, about our climate and the crops we grow, and how I was brought up on a poor hill farm by a father who was a migrant labourer and an illiterate mother. They could understand all that, they themselves came from similar circumstances in Bihar.

We continued our chat while they cut, trimmed, stitched and sewed; the snap of scissors and the whir and tick of the Singers filling in any awkward gaps in our talk.

Then, the unexpected happens.

Amir slips a CD into a ghetto blaster and the room booms with a loud Bollywood soundtrack. He takes my hand and pulls me onto the floor.

He moves gracefully in a slick, gyrating jive while I twist and twirl clumsily and try my best to follow his lead. His two brothers drop their work and join us in the dance. They laugh and clap and spin around me like whirling dervishes while the father sits there good-humoured, his face creased in a big indulgent smile.

In that hemmed-in, clammy room we danced with a hot, sweaty abandon. And in the end when I was breathless and exhausted these three young men took hold of me and raised me on high. And in that moment of unrestrained freedom I felt airborne, buoyantly floating beyond the limits of time. I was back again in those joyous days of early childhood when I asked my father to give me an "*uppity-up into the air*" and he would pick me up, heave me on high and then clasp me securely in his arms as I fell back down.

After that exuberant outburst of dancing and their easy familiarity with me I felt completely at ease with them. What a gracious, agreeable family! I have a feeling that Amir deliberately did that dance just to get me to relax and feel free in their company.

Businesswise they get their orders, mostly, from the local drapers. When someone wants a tailor-made suit or shirt they choose the material in the shop and then the shopkeeper calls the tailor to measure up the customer. It's Amir's job to do this, he's the one with the charm and the winning smile.

In the evening Amir led me back through a maze of narrow, dimly-lit lanes. It was already dark. Here, night falls quickly without the gentle interlude of twilight which we are so accustomed to in our northern climes.

At this time of evening the streets are lined with numerous traders; food vendors; hawkers of shawls and saris; cigarette sellers; dealers in fake designer and pirated DVDs; pedlars carrying bottles of homeopathic concoctions; kerbside cobblers and boot polishers; children selling packets of paper tissue.

This is not a welfare state and people have to make do and survive as best they can by their own endeavours. There are no social handouts, no weekly dole to alleviate the plight of those in need. You have to survive by your own drive and enterprise.

Before I take the metro back to Paharganj we linger for a while at a tea stall drinking chai flavoured with cardamom. From a nearby counter the pungent whiff of spices comes to me from powdery piles of turmeric, cinnamon, nutmeg, cumin, ginger, paprika laid out in rich, vivid displays. A photoshopped Bollywood starlet ogles down at us from a big poster on the facing wall and behind us a small Hindu temple, its deities garlanded with marigolds. An ageing westerner, bald on top but with a tassel of tangled grey hair down his back and wearing a white threadbare dhoti, kneels down and in a show of piety prays aloud to a statue of Ganesh.

"*India is going places,*" is how Amir addresses this sight, a big generous grin on his face.

Just then a scooter weaves and sways through the traffic, horn blaring; an entire family perched on it, the wife sitting side saddle holding a baby, the husband, the only one of them wearing a helmet, a little girl squeezed between him and the handlebars. A common sight here but I can never get used to it. Every time I see this driving recklessness I get anxious and fearful for the safety of those on the scooter or the motorbike. When I told Amir about my dread of those overloaded vehicles he shrugged his shoulders and smiled.

"*This is India. We say no to nothing,*" he said, repeating a zen-like observation that I have heard from other people here. Before we went our separate ways he bought a small Taj Mahal snow globe from a crippled boy selling cheap trinkets and gave it to me.

"*We will meet again, my friend,*" I said and gave him my mobile number as a guarantee. He stood waving to me until I disappeared in the surge of people teeming into the metro station.

10

A Hare Krsna procession comes down the street, a sweet consonance of chant and hand-bells, drums and harmonium. Ten saffron-robed and shaven-headed devotees, they weave their way gracefully through the hubbub and the bustle. They pause in front of the Hari Piorko hotel and in an elated outburst of chanting and dancing they charm myself and other hotel guests into joining them in their holy commotion.

Hare Kṛṣṇa Hare Kṛṣṇa
Kṛṣṇa Kṛṣṇa Hare Hare
Hare Rāma Hare Rāma
Rāma Rāma Hare Hare

The first time I heard the Hare Krsna chant/song/ mantra was on Radio Luxembourg in the summer of 1969. It was sung by George Harrision accompanied by members of the London Radha Krsna Temple. It was a very beguiling sound and I felt then as I do now an urge to dance to it. Now I find myself intoning the words and swaying blissfully to the beat.

Chanting a mantra in a meditative state is known to increase the levels of melatonin in the brain — a secretion produced by the pituitary gland which can induce a sense of well-being and in some cases a spontaneous trance and even visionary ecstasy.

Some sounds are, I believe, vibrationally more subtle than others; more capable, perhaps, to change the neurophysiology of the brain and thus, to alter consciousness, and lure you into rapture.

On that note, so to say, I'm inclined to think of God not as some Almighty Deity presiding over our lives, but more as a creative vibrational force that permeates the whole cosmos. Chanting the Vedic mantras—those subtle energies encased in sound—is a way to avail of this dynamic within oneself.

According to Vedic scriptures we live in the *Kali Yuga*, an age of strife, gloom and despondency, a dark span of 430,000 years of which only 5000 or so of it have already passed. Devotees of Krshna believe that chanting the mantra is a way to ward off and even, undo, some of the evil effects of this dark age. *"Chant and be happy,"* is what these Krsna chanters are urging us to do, impressing upon us, despite the gloom and the doom into which we are born that it's still possible to live in a sublime mode of being.

I'm not so sure that the grimy huddle of street kids that have come to watch and listen would subscribe to this notion. Malnourished, ragged, mistreated, with outstretched hands they compete with the Hare Krsnas for our alms. Our impromptu congregation of chanters do their best to spread around their offerings. When the kids get their share of the charity they give a spirited rendition of the chant but scuttle away when they see a policeman approach. The Hare Krsnas also move down the street, chanting and dancing, leaving me stranded in the *Kali Yuga* and trying to make sense of the screechy babble of being.

11

Today, the penultimate day of my stay here, I visited a sleek glassy, globalized mall close to the Malviya Nagar metro station. Select CITYWALK is boutique-bright consumerism where the old elite and the arrivistes, the monied, the propertied and the privileged meet and socialize. I'm in a small, open-spaced Italian café that serves good coffee. Sitting next to me are two beautifully manicured, facially-peeled, eyebrow-tweezed young women in chic, branded clothes chatting loudly in Hinglish, that fashionable jumble of Hindi and English. They're talking about some swanky do they're going to attend. I can get the drift of what they are saying because the English words stand out like signposts along the path of their chat. The rhyming-chiming Hindi — at least that's how it sounds to me — propels the conversation along at a lively pace. Sipping my coffee I enjoy overhearing their vivacious lingo.

I wanted to engage them in talk but they were too engrossed in their own privileged itineraries to bother with my semantic overtures. Finishing my coffee I left them nibbling at their creamy pastas and talking about "*Asian fusion food*" and "*whitening cream*".

Before leaving the place I took a quick look around at the pricey kitsch and the hyped-up brands and in the bookstore I bought the *Selected Poems* of Kamala Das and a couple of Ruskin Bond's endearingly nostalgic reminiscences of life in the Raj hill stations of his youth.

Waiting for the metro I got thinking about the exotic lexicon that the anglophones seized from the sub-continent, words such as shampoo, verandah, doolally, bungalow, dungarees, pariah, pundit, cashmere and pyjamas, all naturalized now and assimilated to the needs and demands of English.

In the afternoon I visited Akshardham, a monumental temple complex straddling 100 acres on the bank of the Yamuna river. It rises like a paradisal mirage out of the grim, impoverished shantylands by the banks of the holy Yamuna, that murky sludge of sewage and industrial waste; Delhi's main waterway.

Opened in 2005, it is more a tourist attraction than a pilgrimage site. It's really a huge theme park of Hinduism, a Disneyland of consumer spirituality. It has a 15-minute boat ride that takes you through aeons of Indian history. I got the impression from this theatrical voyage that they wanted to play up the idea of a Hindu India that was superior to any of the other creeds or castes that have enriched the cultural diversity of this country. Aside from its pro-Hindu sympathies this utopian project sits awkwardly between being a sacred temple and a corporate concept.

However, it is worth a day trip. One has to admire the bold vision and the single-minded determination it took to achieve this monumentally orchestrated splendour. I spent a few very enjoyable hours strolling around admiring its stone-sculptured pantheon of Hindu deities; its marbled grandiosity; its well choreographed, showcased piety; its beautifully manicured green spaces; its gleaming cleanness; its tranquil lassitude.

It also boasts a range of vegetarian food counters, an ice cream parlour and a well-stocked shop of Akshardhan merchandise.

On the way in, I should add, security is very tight and thorough. You have to deposit your bags and whatever gadgetry you're carrying at the gates. I was surprised when even my notebook, which I held on to after depositing my shoulder bag, was confiscated at one of the check points and I was informed rather brusquely that it was not permitted to carry such an item into the holy shrine.

As I'm leaving Akshardhan, I'm thinking of lines from a poem by K. Satchidanandan, one of India's finest contemporary poets who writes in Malayalam:

> We are the remains of
> an ancient civilisation,
> to land up soon in God's museum

12

Tonight is my last night. I'm in the Everest Bakery Café, close to the hotel, where I often have an evening coffee. I'm reading about a sustained campaign against Tamil writer Perumal Murugan who has earned the ire of various fulminating caste organisations over his novel *One Part Woman* which is set 100 years ago in the author's hometown in Tamil Nadu. The story concerns a childless couple who attend a religious festival where women have consensual sex with men other than their husbands in the hope of conceiving.

The subject matter was deemed sacrilegious and Murugan and his family were forced to flee their home. He has been silenced by ranting fundamentalists. Freedom of expression is under grave threat in India. *Je suis Perumal!*

Sitting beside me is Davitt, a tall, rangy, middle-aged Italian who sells Jew's harps in the bazaars of Delhi and elsewhere. He is also, he tells me, a compulsive collector of matchboxes. He walks the streets, head down in rapt attentiveness on the lookout for a collectible matchbox. He has gathered 600 of them so far, all Indian and different in shape and size. I'm surprised by the multiplicity of designs. He also collects tea strainers. India being an obsessive tea-drinking nation there is no end to the variety of strainers that is to be had.

"Where do you get them?" I asked him.

"I curry favour with people," he said with an evasive chuckle.

Despite the many young backpackers who come here, Paharganj has no vibrant nightlife. By 11pm the shops are shuttered, the street vendors have packed up and gone, the rattle and roar of traffic has subsided and the streets are mostly deserted except for the stray dogs.

Before retiring to my room for the night I took a last walk around familiar haunts, passing a big bony cow guzzling in the rotting garbage and stopping a while at a lovely Hindu temple lit up by golden ghee lamps and fragrant with the reek of sweet incense. It was an uplifting sight and although I didn't "curry any favour" with the deities it raised by spirits.

Tomorrow I will move on to Rajastan and the pink city of Jaipur. Back in my room, thoughts of the open road beckon and quicken my heartbeat.

I await the thrill of a new morning.

Also by The Onslaught Press